Study skills for part-time students

PEARSON
Education

We work with leading authors to develop the strongest educational materials in study skills, bringing cutting-edge thinking and best learning practice to a global market.

Under a range of well-known imprints, including Longman, we craft high-quality print and electronic publications which help readers to understand and apply their content, whether studying or at work.

To find out more about the complete range of our publishing, please visit us on the World Wide Web at:
www.pearsoned.co.uk

Study skills for part-time students

Dr Elizabeth Wilson
Trinity College Carmarthen

Dr Dorothy Bedford
Roehampton University

PEARSON
Longman

Harlow, England • London • New York • Boston • San Francisco • Toronto • Sydney • Singapore • Hong Kong
Tokyo • Seoul • Taipei • New Delhi • Cape Town • Madrid • Mexico City • Amsterdam • Munich • Paris • Milan

Pearson Education Limited
Edinburgh Gate
Harlow
Essex CM20 2JE
England

and Associated Companies throughout the world

Visit us on the World Wide Web at:
www.pearsoned.co.uk

First published 2009

© Pearson Education Limited 2009

ISBN: 978-0-273-71935-9

British Library Cataloguing-in-Publication Data
A catalogue record for this book is available from the British Library

Library of Congress Cataloging-in-Publication Data
A catalog record for this book is available from the Library of Congress

10 9 8 7 6 5 4 3 2 1
13 12 11 10 09

Typeset in 10/12 Helvetica by 30
Printed and bound in Great Britain by Henry Ling Ltd., at the Dorset Press, Dorchester, Dorset

The publisher's policy is to use paper manufactured from sustainable forests.

Brief contents

	Preface	xi
	Acknowledgements	xiii
1	Studying: a life-changing experience	1
2	Personal Development Planning	17
3	Strategies for supporting learning	34
4	Using technology to enhance your learning	54
5	Preparing for research	68
6	Data collection, analysis and presentation	81
7	Quotations, citations and bibliographies	105
8	Techniques for academic writing	120
9	Developing oral presentation skills	143
10	Coping with exams and revision	160
11	After your degree: looking to the future	169
	Bibliography	181
	Glossary	185
	Index	191

Contents

Preface   xi

Acknowledgements   xiii

1 Studying: a life-changing experience   1

Different patterns of work and study   2
Auditing your support network   5
Understanding your learning style   7
Using your workplace as a source of learning   9
Finding a place and time to study   10
Time management   11
Barriers to learning   14
Managing morale and motivation   14
References and further reading   16

2 Personal Development Planning   17

Reflective writing   18
Personal Development Planning (PDP)   22
Producing a professional development portfolio   26
References and further reading   32

3 Strategies for supporting learning   34

Using the Learning Resources Centre   35
Reading effectively   40
Making notes and effective summaries of texts   43
Identifying key points from lectures   47
Learning in seminars, tutorials and groups   50
Looking at available support for improving basic skills   52
References and further reading   53

Contents

4 Using technology to enhance your learning   54

Using the internet and electronic resources   55
The importance of anti-virus software and backups   60
Learning online in the virtual classroom   61
Developing your information technology skills   65
References and further reading   66

5 Preparing for research   68

Preliminary issues   69
Gaining access to workplace data   70
The research process   71
Determining what to research   71
Ethical considerations   75
Reviewing the literature   76
Ensuring validity and reliability   78
Choosing your research sample   79
References and further reading   80

6 Data collection, analysis and presentation   81

Choosing an appropriate methodology   81
Qualitative data collection methods   83
Quantitative data collection methods   87
Analysing qualitative data   93
Analysing quantitative data   98
Presenting the findings   100
Drawing conclusions from the data   102
References and further reading   104

7 Quotations, citations and bibliographies   105

Why you need to cite your sources   106
Quotation in the text   106
How to cite work in the text   109
Using and citing electronic material   110
Footnotes and endnotes   111
Compiling a bibliography   112
Electronic bibliographic management   115
How to avoid plagiarism   116
References and further reading   119

8 Techniques for academic writing 120

Expectations of undergraduate-level writing 121
Understanding generic assessment criteria and marking schemes 122
Managing the writing process for producing assignments 124
Preparing for your first essay 126
Writing for academic purposes – some practical guidance 131
The process of writing your essay 136
Writing reports and dissertations 140
References and further reading 142

9 Developing oral presentation skills 143

Why develop presentation skills? 143
Participating in seminars and tutorials 144
How to plan an effective presentation 145
Using audio-visual aids 150
Using PowerPoint and other technology 155
Making your presentation 156
Group presentations 158
References and further reading 159

10 Coping with exams and revision 160

Stress management 160
Drawing up your revision timetable 161
Important preparation before the exam 164
Techniques for exam success 166
References and further reading 168

11 After your degree: looking to the future 169

Using your careers service 169
Auditing your experiences 170
Writing a professional CV 174
Completing your application 178
References and further reading 180

Bibliography 181

Glossary 185

Index 191

Preface

This book is written for students of all ages and backgrounds who have been accepted onto a degree programme, but who carry additional responsibilities such as employment. Universities and colleges are increasingly composed of students who have a range of entry qualifications and diverse experiences. We recognise that trying to manage the demands of study with the responsibilities and pressure of work places you under considerable strain at times. Indeed, much of our own study has been undertaken while working full time and juggling other responsibilities.

In writing *Study Skills for Part-time Students*, we have used the unique experiences of a range of successful students from diverse graduate courses and higher education establishments, all of whom have combined paid employment with studying. We are extremely grateful to them for being prepared to share with us their accumulated wisdom. We feel that this has given us an insight into strategies they used to support their learning and we will return to their comments throughout the text, in the belief that reading about their experiences will give authenticity to what we say.

We will equip you with the study skills to enable you to move from novice student to successful graduate. We have included chapters which focus on the skills of reading effectively, making notes, academic writing, giving presentations, research, and examinations and other forms of assessment, all of which are required for your successful study. In addition we have considered ways you can understand yourself and support your learning, use your workplace, plan your future development, boost your morale and keep yourself motivated, manage your time and use technology, and prepare for life beyond your degree. Although the chapters follow sequentially through the experiences you will meet as a student, our intention is that you will be able to return to topics as you need them throughout your degree.

We wish you well with your study.

Dr Elizabeth Wilson

Dr Dorothy Bedford

Acknowledgements

We would particularly like to acknowledge the help of Niki Consiglio, Paula Field, Patrick Forbes-Ritte, Margaret Grogan, Emma Harper, Caroline Hart, Debbie Nathan, Jackie Nolan, Frances Pennell-Buck, Clair Rauso, Anneca Robinson, Lynda Rondeau, LisaMarie Sheppard, Subiratha Sivakumaran, Julie Smith and Sally Stanton, in addition to our many other students who contributed to this book. It has been a great privilege to work with them and listen to their advice.

Throughout the text we have recommended a range of electronic sources of information and are very grateful to the Higher Education Academy which has given us permission to draw on its work.

In addition, we thank Oxford Brookes University Business School for permission to use an example of their marking scheme and Anglia Ruskin University for permission to use their generic assessment criteria and marking standards

We would like to acknowledge the support and encouragement of many colleagues at Roehampton University, Trinity College Carmarthen and the Open University whose insights have contributed to this book. We thank our families and, in particular, Peter Davies and Charles Bedford for their support.

Dr Elizabeth Wilson

Dr Dorothy Bedford

Publisher's acknowledgements

We are grateful to the following for permission to reproduce copyright material:

Figures: Figure on page 102 from New partnerships for learning: teachers and teaching assistants working together in schools – the way forward, *Journal of Education for Teaching*, 34:2, 137–50. (Wilson, E. and Bedford, D., 2008). Reproduced with permission from Taylor & Francis via the copyright clearance center (www.copyright.com); Figure 8.1 adapted from Anglia Ruskin Generic Assessment Criteria and Marking Standards (levels 0-4). Reproduced with permission from Anglia Ruskin University; Figure 8.2 criteria is adapted from the Foundation Degree in Communication programme offered at Oxford Brookes University Business School. Reproduced with permission.

Acknowledgements

Text: Extract on page 2 adapted from *Work-based Learning: Illuminating the Higher Education Landscape, Report by KSA Partnership for The Higher Education Academy,* The Higher Education Academy (Nixon, I., Smith, K., Stafford, S. and Camm, S., 2006) Figure 4, p. 43. reproduced with permission.

In some instances we have been unable to trace the owners of copyright material, and we would appreciate any information that would enable us to do so.

1 Studying: a life-changing experience

This book aims to enable those of you who are working as well as studying not only to survive and achieve your qualifications but also to enjoy the life-changing experience. Not so long ago most students would be those who had gained appropriate qualifications at school and automatically went on to university to further their learning; most of whom would have had their fees paid and be awarded funding. With the increasing need for a more qualified workforce and the recognition that learning can take place at anytime in a person's life, non-traditional patterns of studying are becoming the norm.

The one unifying factor for each of you reading this book is that you have, for one reason or another, decided to undertake further study in order to gain additional qualifications. The student body in most universities and colleges is now made up of people of all ages and backgrounds with a range of entry qualifications, many of whom carry additional responsibilities such as employment. Indeed, a survey conducted by Woodley (2004) into the incomes of and costs incurred by higher education students revealed that 83 per cent of part-timers were in paid employment.

This chapter covers:

- different patterns of work and study
- auditing your support network
- understanding your learning style
- finding a place and time to study
- time management
- barriers to learning
- managing morale and motivation.

Different patterns of work and study

There are a number of reasons why students work at the same time as studying:

- some are intending to change their careers or advance their chances in the workplace;
- some will be hoping to gain skills and knowledge which will be useful in their present role;
- some want to improve their personal and professional practice in the place where they are already employed;
- some will be learning in order to improve the effectiveness of their workplace;
- others will be using employment to fund their studies.

For those of you involved in work-based learning, Nixon *et al.* (2006) described the provision for learning as a series of continuums as follows:

Provider identifies needs	→ Employers and learners identify needs
Develops generic knowledge and skills	→ Develops technical knowledge and skills
Creates new knowledge	→ Transfers existing knowledge
Work focused	→ Work relevant
Fixed schedule of delivery	→ Flexible schedule of delivery
Learning in the workplace	→ Learning away from the workplace
Support is programme centred	→ Support is learner centred
Learning support provided by provider	→ Learning support provide by employer
Wholly recognised by a professional body	→ No element recognised by a professional body
Assessment focuses on knowledge	→ Assessment focuses on skills
Provider undertakes assessment	→ Employer and/or learner assesses
Wholly accredited by provider	→ No element accredited
Evaluate quality of learning experience	→ Evaluate impact on learner development and organisation

When you read what our students say about their decision to study you will note not only their range of reasons but also their variety of backgrounds.

Case Study

Anneca, who graduated, may at first seem like your idea of a typical student. She said:

'I have always wanted to become a teacher and so, from an early age, I knew that the route into teaching was only possible with a classified degree. This then made me go on to university to study for a BA in Education with English Literature. I was

▶

able to work part time during the three years and at one point I held down three jobs which, looking back, did affect my studies. My family also relied heavily on me. However, looking back, I now realise that I made the choices while studying to take on the commitments and responsibilities. So it was my choice to work due to financial circumstances and family responsibilities, however, everybody is different and has various commitments.'

Case Study

Sally said:

'I completed GCE 'O' level exams during the 1960s and continuing on for further/higher education was not a possibility. I went into the world of work. I have worked for the same company for the last 23 years and have worked my way up from Clerical Officer to Office Manager and am now a PA . . . My two children have grown up and left home, so I had some flexibility in my home life.'

Case Study

Jackie also saw an opportunity to gain qualifications:

'In my role as Senior Administrative Officer at a small primary school there had been very little opportunity for professional development as courses aimed at admin staff were very rare. As soon as I saw the flyer for the Foundation Degree in Educational Administration I felt that I finally had the opportunity to develop my skills and knowledge in the same way as classroom-based staff.'

Case Study

Caroline noted that it was:

'. . . a requirement of my current role . . . as a compliance officer . . . having not attended university and gone straight to work from 'O' Levels and in full-time employment. This is a relatively new role and therefore there is a lot to learn – the demands are high.'

Case Study

Debbie also had to undertake study:

'. . . to meet the requirements of the National Minimum Standards for Care Homes to become a Registered Care Home Manager. We were extremely busy as owners of three homes and were involved on a daily basis. My partner and I did all the accounts, finances, shopping and regular visits to the Homes to solve problems and so on.'

The employment patterns of our respondents are represented in the table below. Can you see where you fit in? We have added a few riders which may be of help to you.

Different patterns of work and study

Employment	Study/teaching
Full-time employment	Taught course during evenings and at weekends. Your employer may give you some study time during the day to meet deadlines.
Full-time employment	Time released for daytime course (especially where study is a requirement of your employer). Again additional time may be given on occasions.
Part-time employment (daytime)	Course attendance and study fitted around each other. Employers may be prepared to be flexible if course requirements or arrangements change.
Part-time employment (evening or night)	Course attendance during the day (yes, it has been done. Look below at what Patrick said).
Flexible working	Course attendance may take precedence with work fitted in. This may be more suited to self-employment or piece-work.

Case Study

Patrick said:

'The only way I could fund my studies was to take a full-time course, this was the principal reason for full-time work and full-time Uni . . .

I had no experience of intense study. I also had a full-time job in mental health on a shift rota. I discussed my needs with management who were helpful in allowing me to transfer to night shift . . . from 21:15 to 08:15. The final challenge was getting to Uni for lectures at 09:00. Careful planning to arrange shifts on days when I did not have early morning lectures alleviated some of the stress . . . I had to block out periods in my diary that allowed me to get off shift, wash and change, go to Uni, put in 5–6 hours of lectures, breaks, lunch, seminars and home, tea and then sleep until 20:45 and return to work.

Diary planning is essential, checking lecture programmes and arranging shifts to fit around them. I would give my employer a list of 'request days' when I would prefer not to be at work. As I asked well in advance my employers were very accommodating and I seldom had to ask colleagues to cover for me. You need to stick to the plan rigidly, this sometimes meant forceful rebuttal of last minute changes to rotas. You have to be in control all of the time. You have to become selfish in your commitment and focused on your aims.'

The decision to work at the same time as studying is not something to be taken lightly. Indeed, a study by Long *et al.* (2006) investigating the first year experiences of students in higher education in the UK, noted that, when students were carrying out more than 12 hours of paid employment they were much more likely to cite financial problems and the demands of employment while studying, as reasons for not continuing their studies. When the number of worked hours exceeded 18, emotional difficulties and the needs of dependants became a major factor in the decision to drop out. A study by McMillan (2005) suggests that the detrimental effect of part-time employment on younger students was reached when working exceeded nine hours per week.

> **Case Study**
>
> The last word here should go to Anneca:
>
> 'I would advise anyone not to try and juggle too many things at one go and if you have to work, try and find the right balance between the two. It is easy to get caught up with the working life whilst earning money and forget about the most important thing of gaining and studying for your degree. I made the mistake of taking on too many responsibilities and thought that I would be able to manage the two, but if you don't find the right balance, your studies are affected.'

Auditing your support network

To have come this far, you will already have thought seriously about the course of study you are embarking on. This next stage is vital in helping you to succeed. Research has shown that students identified making friends as a crucial element of a positive higher education experience: something that is more difficult to achieve for those who are 'commuter students' (Yorke and Longden, 2008).

Our personal circumstances are unique and varied, but few of us choose to be totally alone. Most of us have family and friends. These people who are closely connected to you are your support network; similarly the students working alongside you and your workmates can also give support.

> **Case Study**
>
> Jackie, Paula and Sally offer their experiences:
>
> 'Realise that you can only achieve success with dedication and commitment, you have to be a bit selfish when organising your time. Have a long conversation with family members because without their understanding and cooperation, completing the course would be very difficult. Make good friends with your classmates; swapping ideas and research hints is invaluable. During my course we would meet on a regular basis to compare assignments and give each other advice on layout, content and so on. We were also in regular contact via e-mail. We still are! It took us a couple of months to realise that we were not in competition with each other and we became good friends.'
>
> 'I would advise anyone studying alongside other major commitments to think very carefully about the time needed to complete work. Everything seems to take twice as long as you think it will, even when there are no obstacles in your way. Ensure that your family are on your side and understand just how much of your time and energy studying will take up. They are the people who will be making the sacrifices alongside you.'
>
> 'If you have older children and an understanding husband, use them. Lots of little jobs done by others soon add up, leaving you more time to study.'

You will have to sit down and discuss your decision with your family and friends. The more they understand what you are undertaking, the more supportive they may be. Others you live with could, for example, do more of the chores, especially during your peak study times. By agreeing some ground rules at the beginning of your course you should be able to share out some of your current responsibilities. Sometimes spending more money will save you time, like getting food deliveries online, or employing someone to help in the house or garden. Consider any affordable options that will make your life easier.

Case Study

Emma suggests:

'Schedule in 'family time' to your work schedule so they don't feel left out. I think we value what we do together as a family more now.'

You should not underestimate the impact that your goal will have on those around you. For example, try not to lose contact with your friends. It is hard enough to stay connected to people with our already busy lives. A number of our students also said that by studying they acted as a role model for their children.

Forming a study network with students on your course is crucial. It can be informal and may happen as a result of taking a coffee after the lecture. Even if you commute and need to leave quite promptly, phone, text and e-mail are excellent substitutes.

Case Study

Lynda advises:

'Use the internet and set up an e-mail group. It helps motivation and keeps you on task if you are struggling.'

Be prepared to make the first move: if you wait to be asked it might be assumed you are not interested.

Case Study

Patrick highlighted his 'study group' as one of the most important strategies to overcome obstacles getting in the way of study:

'The 'study group' consolidated our learning, working, study preparation and research periods. It became the focal point of our aims and goals. At times the group would meet for a whole weekend doing little else than study, eat, drink, sleep and more study. The inward focus cemented friendships based on common goals and aspirations and excluded peripheral distractions. Fanatical? Yes, we were. We fed off each other's commitment; when we felt down, the others encouraged.'

Understanding your learning style

An important part of preparing for any kind of study is to identify how you learned what you already know. In that way you can build on success and learn from any failure. For at least the last century, researchers, psychologists and teachers have proposed theories of learning and suggested teaching styles to assist learning. More recently there has been a specific interest in adult learning. But, in spite of the number of books, journal articles and research papers devoted to the subject, we are still some way from understanding the key differences in learning as a child and learning as an adult. We also have to be careful not to assume that theories about adult learning apply equally to everyone. Differences of class, culture, ethnicity, personality, cognitive style, knowing and understanding, learning patterns, life experiences and gender among adults are more significant than the fact that we are not children or adolescents. We have tried to bear this in mind while writing this book and offer a selection of ideas from the theorists to help you understand yourself. There will be times when you disagree with something that we have suggested. We see this as a positive step; it shows that you are developing as a critical reader.

Research suggests that there are three levels of learning:

- **Cognition**: knowing and understanding. For example, you watched the demonstration and now know how to create tables and charts in a spreadsheet package.
- **Conception**: deep understanding which can be recalled. For example, three weeks, or even a year later, you can still create tables and could do it again unaided.
- **Application**: understanding and use of the knowledge. For example, not only have you learned this skill, you have added to that knowledge and are able to explain it to someone else.

Ideally we are always working towards the application level.

We also need to think about the ways we gain knowledge. We have a tendency to assume that all learning is conscious and the result of applying ourselves in school or college. But what about learning to ride a bicycle, for instance? Much of that was quite unconscious; maybe we watched someone carefully. That type of learning is referred to as tacit. Procedural knowledge is what you gain from doing something repeatedly. Explicit knowledge is what you learn in your lectures or by reading a book. You can see that to be successful you need to be learning in all three ways.

Additionally, the way we process information can be categorised using the acronym VARK:

- **Visual**: those who learn through seeing.
- **Auditory**: those who take in information through listening.
- **Read/write**: those who prefer the written word.
- **Kinaesthetic**: those who learn best when active.

If you want to find out more about this there are several websites where you can complete a VARK profile. You might recognise the way you process information or see that you fall into more than one category; what is important is that you begin to understand yourself as a learner. Learning can take place for you in a variety of ways other than through reading and writing. However, as you know, most of the emphasis is on reading and writing, and this can lead you to suppose that only those who are good at that way of processing knowledge are intelligent. In this respect it is worth considering Howard Gardner's theory of multiple intelligences.

What Gardner claimed, in 1983, was that intelligence is not only about being academically clever, that is, good at mathematics, reading and writing, but also about using life experiences. To support his argument he used examples of other sorts of knowledge that people acquire, sometimes to an exceptional standard, without necessarily having any academic learning at all. On the basis of his discoveries Gardner proposed that there is a range of different intelligences. In his original theory there were seven; the last one in the list below is a recent addition and it is likely more will be added as his evidence accumulates. Each of these intelligences can be linked to preferences in the way you process and use information, and you can see they have similarities to the theories described above.

Gardner's intelligences are:

- **Linguistic/verbal:** The ability to use language in written and oral forms.
- **Logical/mathematical:** The ability to reason logically and manipulate numbers.
- **Visual/spatial:** The ability to recognise and produce visual images.
- **Kinaesthetic:** The ability to coordinate the body and use it to express and achieve goals.
- **Musical:** The ability to recognise and produce music.
- **Naturalist:** The ability to recognise and interact with the natural world.
- **Interpersonal:** The ability to understand the motives, emotional states and intentions of others.
- **Intrapersonal:** The ability to understand one's own motives, characteristics, strengths and weaknesses.

Considerable research has been carried out, notably by Peter Jarvis (1992), into adult learners' recollections of the way they learn. His research suggests that the way you confront a learning experience determines what you learn. He found that there are three states:

1. Non-learning:
   - making the same mistakes even when they are pointed out;
   - thinking that you already know what is being taught;
   - thinking it is not worth paying attention;
   - rejecting what you have been taught.

2. Non-reflective learning:
   - changing learning behaviour and gaining new skills without really understanding what you have done and why.

3. Reflective learning:
   - deep changes in understanding as a result of reflecting objectively, relating the learning to previous experience. You will find more about reflective learning in chapter 2.

Clearly it is better to be a reflective learner. You will notice that reference to reflection and reflecting on your learning appears throughout the text.

The ideas of David Kolb (1984) have probably had more influence on how people think about learning than any other writer's. He visualised four phases in what he called a 'learning cycle' as stages which we work through:

- **Concrete experience**: carrying out the work.
- **Observation and reflection**: reflecting on the experience.
- **Forming abstract concepts**: thinking about what helped you learn and what got in the way.
- **Testing in new situations**: planning study tasks taking account of the way you prefer to learn.

Using your workplace as a source of learning

If you are undertaking work-based learning, see if there is someone at work who would be prepared to act as your mentor. The ideal mentor is usually a more experienced colleague who already holds a qualification at a similar or more advanced level, and who has practical experience of the job. This may be your line manager, but not necessarily. You need to find a person with whom you can be open and honest about any difficulties you may be experiencing.

Mentors have a key role in facilitating work-based learning and can use their knowledge of the workplace to help access information that can assist in your studies. They can also help you to make the link between the theoretical knowledge you acquire from academic study and your professional practice and put you in touch with individuals who have 'expert knowledge'. Regular meetings with your mentor can focus on making these links and encourage you to reflect on your personal and professional development.

Your workplace may have provided you with a range of experiences which have contributed to your learning.

Case Study   Jackie reminds us not to overlook the workplace as a source of information:

'Use your own experiences, at work and in life, to help build your knowledge of a subject. I have linked assignments such as my dissertation to events and strategies being implemented at work. This helped my professional development and made the subject more relevant and interesting for me.'

Finding a place and time to study

Finding a place that is conducive to study is important. The ideal solution is a quiet room where you will not be disturbed, but not everyone is fortunate enough to have this space. If you are able to have a designated area at home consider how your circumstances match up against the following checklist:

- desk or table, large enough to spread out your books and files and accommodate a laptop or PC if necessary;
- comfortable chair which supports your back and is designed for use with a computer if appropriate;
- adequate heating and ventilation – you do not want to be so warm that you doze off or so cold that you cannot concentrate;
- appropriate lighting – preferably natural light and a reading lamp you can turn on at night;
- storage space, a bookcase or cupboard where you can easily put your work away, and a waste paper basket;
- access to a computer. This is ideal but you may be able to use a computer at your workplace or college. If you need to share a home computer with others then access times need to be negotiated;
- good supply of stationery items such as coloured pens, pencils, highlighter pens, ruler, calculator, Post-it® notes, stapler, hole punch, files, dividers and paper.

Although you may have negotiated with members of your family to have uninterrupted study time you may need to hang a 'DO NOT DISTURB' sign on the door or take the phone off the hook. Research shows that most students study best in a quiet environment. If you find that the radio or TV improves your mood, keep the volume low. With experience you will be able to decide where and how you study best.

Time management

You have already considered the way in which building a support network can help and have thought about how you learn best. Now it is really important to organise your time. Yes, we mean planning. Experience shows that a lot of time can be wasted because we think it is not long enough to be useful. There are many different ways of managing your time, so there are no hard and fast rules. What is important for you is to take some control and avoid the stress that comes from panicking about being left behind and do what works for you. Caroline confessed that she was not sure she 'identified any effective strategies, deadlines focused the mind', but this may not work for you.

Try mapping out your week a day at a time like a timetable. Put in the things you cannot avoid such as lecture periods, time at work, domestic commitments and so on and remember to factor in travelling time. Consider when you work best; are you a 'lark' or an 'owl'? It is no good planning your longest study periods at night if you will be too tired to concentrate; it might be better for you to set the alarm and get up before everyone else. Then map in some quality time; partners, children and friends do deserve a little of you and it does help to have treats to look forward to.

Case Study	Always use opportunities. Sally used the time when her partner's friends came round to watch football 'to get my books out and do some research or writing'. She said 'I would never have finished the course if I had not used all my spare time for my studies'.

Caroline said: 'Map out your study/work, include any events such as holidays/birthdays and so on and then try to stick to the plan. Obviously the unplanned happens so factor in some contingency.' This was reinforced by Jackie 'I said lack of time would be a threat to my studies, but never thought it would be to such an extent. I have also found that even when you plan the time the unexpected will happen, such as illness, and your plans will be thrown up in the air . . . I don't believe you can prevent the obstacles from getting in the way of your study, you simply need to be very focused and driven. I have been determined to not only complete the course but to do well.' And she did.

Covey *et al.*'s (1994) theories of time management have been influential in many successful businesses. Although you could argue that study is not the same as business, all businesses are made up of individuals, and work or study are both demands which have to be met. He proposed that you consider the demands on your time and decide into which of four quarters of a quadrant they belong. The first quarter represented those things which were both urgent and important; the second were those that were were not urgent but important; the third quadrant represented those things which were urgent but not important and, the fourth, those that were neither important nor urgent. The ideal was that we should spend most of our time on tasks in the second quarter, the 'Quadrant of Quality.' The argument being, that many important activities, such as revising for examinations and planning for assignments, only become urgent through procrastination or because we don't do enough planning. By the time the activity becomes urgent, it transfers to the first quarter and this causes us stress.

We do, of course, need to spend some time on urgent important tasks such as dealing with imminent deadlines and unforeseen crises, in the 'Quadrant of Necessity'. However, by investing time on important but not urgent tasks we are taking control of the situation, and gradually the need for urgency diminishes. Covey suggests that the third quarter is the 'Quadrant of Deception' because we are meeting other people's priorities and expectations, rather than our own. Here things are urgent, but not important, so why are we doing them? Usually the answer is because they are important to someone else. As for the final quarter where the activities are neither urgent nor important, Covey describes this as the 'Quadrant of Waste'. Taking good care of yourself fits in to the second quarter and not, as you might think, into the final one.

ACTIVITY 1 Time management

Keep a diary for a week identifying how you spend your time. Include your weekends and all activities from waking to sleeping. You may find it helpful to carry it around with you. Estimate each activity to the nearest quarter of an hour. Then consider where you spend most of your time. Draw the four quarters and use Covey's time management headings and then write in where each major activity fits on the importance/urgency grid. What does this tell you about how you are currently managing your time?

Now you have looked at the way you are using your time, consider how you might gain 'extra' time (bearing in mind how you work best and your energy levels) such as:

- Getting up earlier every day and perhaps studying for an hour before everyone else is awake. Debbie confessed to getting up before the crack of dawn (sometimes at 4 or 5am) to do coursework in peace and quiet before the normal day began at 8am.
- Planning to work on a number of evenings a week, but not every night.
- Finding time to study in between other activities. As Sally said: 'I stored all my work on my computer at home, at work and on my memory stick, so I could work when I could.' Consider using your travelling time on public transport as well. This is rarely going to give you high quality study time but it has the additionally benefit of keeping your ideas 'alive' until you can get down to longer study.

ACTIVITY 2 Planning

Make notes about the last period you spent studying. Ask yourself:

- How long did I take to get down to the task?
- Did I spend time worrying rather than tackling what needed to be done?

▶

- Was I distracted by other people or unrelated tasks?
- Did I make a plan or list what I was going to do?
- Did I prioritise and complete important work first?
- How long was I able to concentrate on the task?
- Was I studying at the best time for me?

Not only is it important to plan week by week, but you do need an oversight of the demands of the whole year. This way you will be able to identify where the crisis points are likely to be, so that you can plan ahead. Identify beginnings and endings of taught time, exam and module submission dates, presentations and so on and then map in domestic commitments – birthdays, anniversaries, holidays and short breaks. You will need to keep this somewhere prominent when you are planning your weekly schedule.

ACTIVITY 3 Priorities

Consider your priorities for the week ahead and map them on to your weekly plan. First consider the tasks you need to complete, then prioritise them using Covey's headings:

- Look at the reading you need to do before a particular lecture and schedule this in. It is clearly much better to complete any recommended reading before your lecture. In that way you will have a good understanding of the points your lecturer is making, rather than trying to catch up afterwards, or ignoring the reading completely.
- Look at any assignments coming up that you need to read around. Often your lecturers will give you an idea of how to tackle a particular piece of coursework. Further reading afterwards will consolidate your ideas and help you plan for essays and other assignments.
- Plan for work that is due in shortly. Organise these pieces of work, such as essays and seminar papers, into smaller and less daunting chunks. Remember, you need to allocate significant amounts of time to writing and redrafting. Writing tasks need the highest quality time and should be attempted when you are most productive, although you may be able to fit your smaller preparation tasks into 'down time'.
- Ensure you do not neglect any of your modules, so make sure you complete something to contribute to each of your areas of study, rather than just the one with the most pressing deadline.

Time when you are able to focus solely on your studies is really important for you. You do not want to spend high quality time thinking about what you should be doing. There is a danger that if you spend too long planning it can turn into procrastination.

You do need to consider what needs to be done before you start each work session; what must be done without fail comes first; what would be useful comes next; then decide if any tasks you considered as urgent but not important are now important and should be completed. You should discard any tasks which are neither urgent, nor important. All our respondents recommend careful planning and not leaving anything to the last minute. When you have finished your work session, reward yourself.

Case Study	Heather, who graduated with a distinction, said: 'Start early so you can take a break if necessary. Sometimes enforced breaks mean you are more focused when you return to the work.'

Barriers to learning

According to a survey the two potentially strong influences likely to make students consider withdrawing from their courses are difficulty in balancing academic and other commitments and inadequate knowledge of their programme before enrolling (Woodley, 2004). These two factors alone can constitute a significant barrier to your learning. It is going to be very important for you to see not only ways in which the demands of your studies can be accommodated with your other commitments, but also that you have selected the right course. Caroline advises: 'Only undertake study if you are truly committed; you will find every excuse not to if you are not.' All our contributors have said in various ways that you need to be realistic, committed and some say 'selfish'. 'Be prepared to work long hours and feel tired [but] don't give up, get yourself organised, try to stay on top of the work and don't be afraid to ask for help.'

Managing morale and motivation

As already mentioned, research suggests that our adult learning is quite different from when we were young. Maybe this is a good thing because some of you may carry quite negative memories of your earlier learning experiences. Making a success of what is an exciting opportunity is therefore very important for you. Starting a degree is nearly always exciting; your confidence has been boosted by getting a place on the course, you have bought the books, organised your work space and things could not be better. Be prepared, however, for times when your morale will be low. There is nothing more damaging to your studies. It can make you doubt yourself so much that you find you are just sitting and staring at your work. Worse still you cannot concentrate on your studies and look for more pleasant things to do; or even decide not to continue your degree.

Low morale is a lot more common than you may think and can be caused by a whole range of factors:

- change to your routines, such as different hours, new travel arrangements to organise;
- too much information to absorb, such as new routes, new surroundings, new names and faces, texts to buy, rooms to find;

- cultural changes to make, such as being part of a very large organisation, forming different types of relationships with peers and tutors, new ideas;
- loss of confidence in your ability to meet the standards needed to complete the degree;
- not feeling in control of your learning;
- not feeling that you are part of the academic community; you fear that your ideas, your way of speaking, your appearance and so on set you apart. You want to 'belong';
- you feel that your studies are separating you from your family and friends;
- feeling that the work is far too difficult and you do not know where to begin;
- being unable to make any sense of a set text you have been asked to read;
- technology letting you down, your printer stops working for no apparent reason;
- a friend or family member needs you and you have work to finish for a deadline;
- a tutor, a part of a course, or a set text is really boring;
- you get a poor mark for an assignment;
- you worry unnecessarily about a slightly lower grade than usual and start to get obsessed by your marks;
- it is all becoming too much of a routine – this is often referred to as the 'midway blues'.

Case Study

Jenny said: 'I went to university at the age of 24, having been in full-time employment since I left school at 16. I found returning to education very difficult and university is, of course, so different to school. I disliked the lack of structure and discipline; I was not confident in managing my time and knowing what I should be doing and when. I was extremely conscientious and wanted to do well but I became depressed and felt I could not continue, despite good exam/assessment results. I felt completely overwhelmed.'

The following is a list of things identified by our students which lifted their morale. Sometimes it is only a case of changing perspective and looking at the same thing in a different way. Think positively:

- having the satisfaction of finishing a set task or a difficult text, especially if you finish before the deadline;
- being proud of a result which was better than expected;
- getting your work organised and planning your time;
- focusing on what you have achieved so far;
- learning about something which is really interesting;
- realising you know enough to express a point of view, and feeling confident enough to do so;
- being brave enough to present a paper and then being praised;

Reflective writing

Reflective writing provides an opportunity for you to think critically about past events and your own learning journey. We are told by our new degree students that they often find this a difficult task, as it is different from other forms of writing they have done before. Reflective writing offers the opportunity for you to challenge yourself about what you do. It also gives you the objectivity to do things differently and better, without seeing problems as a result of personal inadequacy. Keeping a reflective journal is challenging, but can help you to develop a scholarly approach to your practice and to learning. This is an essential feature both for being effective as a workplace professional and for studying for your degree.

Setting the parameters

As we suggested above, when used effectively, reflective writing will support you in making personal sense of a diverse set of experiences. This is particularly important if learning is to be incorporated into everyday practice as it is in the workplace. However, because you are writing about your personal experiences, there are some ground rules and boundaries that need to be set at the beginning of the process. In all cases, before you start to write you will need to know who will see your reflective journal, and if it will be assessed as part of your qualification.

ACTIVITY 1 Before you begin

Check that you have the answers to the following questions before you start your journal:

- Is the journal part of my assessed work? If so, what are the assessment criteria? Is there a word limit?
- Who will see this writing? Will this work be seen by a second marker or the external examiner, or is it just for me?
- Is it acceptable to present handwritten work? If you use a standard diary it is likely your entries will be handwritten unless you have a PDA (Personal Digital Assistant) or use a package like Microsoft Outlook®.
- What guidelines are there for content? As you are employed and studying, is there a balance to be struck between reflection on your academic and workplace learning?

In the literature regarding reflective practice, the work of Donald Schön (1983) is most often cited. He writes about reflection having two key components: 'reflection on action', a retrospective activity looking back after any particular event or task, and evaluating current skills, competencies, knowledge and professional practice. 'Reflection in action', a more dynamic process which takes place during the task or event, and which helps to improve performance by adjusting what we do. What you might term 'thinking on your feet'. This work has been extended by Cowan (1998) who adds 'reflection for action', where you reflect on and learn from previous activities to inform the planning for the next. Consider these ideas in your own journal, and decide at what point you are actually reflecting.

What could your reflective writing include?

There are many ways of structuring a reflective journal. However, in all cases your tutor is likely to want to see:

- an analysis of what went well, why it worked and what you achieved. They will not want a straight description of what happened with no analysis. However, you may need to be descriptive to briefly set the context;
- what could have been better and how you would achieve this. Here you are expected to be honest, knowing what went wrong shows that you have learned from the situation. Try to explain the issue rather than offering excuses or blaming others; Margaret suggests you 'question things objectively as you do them';
- any links you can make between the theory you have been studying and what happened in practice;
- what you have learned and will do differently in the future. This could be in the format of a formal action plan (see the final section of this chapter). It could be a brief informal note about the changes you would make and how you will know if you have improved.

> **Case Study** Susan suggests you try to 'think about something after it happened, what you would have done better or differently', and Julie advises: 'Question everything that you do – What? How? Did it work?'

The important thing is to start to write your thoughts down; you can edit your ideas later. Lara suggests you 'look into all aspects of your life. Be clear and write your reflective journal as soon as possible after the incident.' To start you off we have suggested an agenda you may like to follow. As you become more familiar with this type of writing, other questions will come to mind and you may prefer to think more creatively.

ACTIVITY 2 Reflect

Your first task is to identify something to reflect on. Are you concerned about something at work or at college, or are you particularly pleased or interested in an activity? Does a critical incident stand out? For example, when we did this exercise with our students, a number of them chose to reflect on their feelings on the first day of the course. Now ask yourself a series of questions; these may start you off:

▶

- What happened? What is the current problem or issue? Here you can briefly describe the context and use descriptive rather than reflective writing. It is useful to consider what you were responsible for.
- How did you feel? What were your assumptions? Could your assumptions be challenged?
- How did others feel or react? Did they react in the same way or differently from you? Did their reaction affect you?
- Reflect on the actual outcome – what worked well? Why did it work in this way?
- What were the negative points? What were the reasons for them?
- What could be done differently by you and by others next time? Who could help? How would you summarise what you have learned from this experience?

Case Study

Christina suggests you 'pick an issue and thrash it out. Pick yourself to pieces and argue with yourself. Put in strategies and evaluate their outcomes in further reflections.' Jane advises that 'the art of being reflective is to look at yourself, your weaknesses, good points, personal achievements, disappointments and summarise them. This way you create a diary of growth and personal development.'

Shaping the journal to suit you – possible ideas for structure

In the form of a diary

Many students find it helpful to buy a large diary or A4 hardback notebook and to write about their work on a regular basis. This idea works well as a personal learning journey, tracking and documenting an evolving understanding of your work and your study. There are advantages to this method. If you use this as your one and only diary, make sure you have it with you all the time. Robbie suggests you 'write your diary at work, get a hardback book and carry it around.' However, you do need to ensure that your writing is reflective rather than descriptive. One way around this is to note down incidents as they occur, in your diary, and then critically consider the issues later, following the guidelines in the exercise you have just completed. Helen advises 'don't be descriptive when writing your journal. Go deep into what you are writing, ask yourself what can you do about this?'

In terms of issues and themes

Another approach would be to see if you could integrate different parts of your degree in a holistic manner. A danger of undertaking any modular qualification is that the subjects are seen separately. This approach could be an opportunity for you to see your area of study as a whole and identify common themes across the modules.

One interesting way to organise your journal might be to focus on a reading which is part of your course and again use it to identify themes which will give headings for the sections of your journal rather than using dates. You can experiment with this approach by using the following questions to guide your reflection:

- How does this connect with an aspect of my practice at work or personal views?
- What could I change in relation to this?
- What would happen if I did?

An analysis of critical incidents

A critical incident is an event which impacted either directly on your professional practice, or indirectly on the way you perceive something about your career.

ACTIVITY 3 Analyse events

Imagine the organisation you work for is about to come under new ownership and restructuring is inevitable:

- Describe the incident as objectively as possible.
- What were the assumptions that you were operating with?
- Is there another way to see this event?
- How do the two explanations compare?
- What could you do differently?

A reflection on your own personal development

A journal could provide a critical reflection on your learning at work, development activities or on the degree itself. It can be very helpful to focus on feedback you have received on your assignments. Subiratha suggests you 'write down your thoughts and feelings after each session, and about anything new you learn in your workplace or from your reading.' If you go through a performance review or appraisal at work, reflect on the perceptions of others.

If you are keeping a professional development journal for assessment you will probably be asked to produce a separate ongoing action plan, which is described in the last section of this chapter. However, if this is not part of the requirement for your particular degree you may wish to consider the following questions in your journal:

- What do I need to do to improve the quality of what I do?
- What might I do instead of what I do now?

- What am I doing well that I could develop further?
- What innovation could I introduce?
- What other development activities should I be seeking?

Personal Development Planning (PDP)

Resources for Personal Development Planning

All higher education institutions are expected to provide a form of Personal Development Planning (PDP) for their students, so your first port of call should be your own university. A number of HE institutions have produced electronic PDP systems. There is also a wide range of resources available on the internet which will be discussed further in this chapter. The sites mentioned in the section on e-portfolios will also provide a useful starting point. In addition you may wish to identify your preferred learning style, as mentioned in the first chapter, by working through the questionnaire on **www.learning-styles-online.com**. You should also look at the site called Skills4Study which provides PDP resources for students (**www.palgrave. com/skills4study/pdp/**).

Some ideas for developing your own PDP

Complete a SWOT analysis

SWOT stands for Strengths, Weaknesses, Opportunities and Threats. Carry out an initial diagnosis of your strengths and areas for further development. What opportunities exist for you to resolve weaknesses and demonstrate your strengths? What threats are there to prevent your development?

ACTIVITY 4 SWOT Analysis

Complete a SWOT analysis using the questions below as a prompt and including any more thoughts of your own. Consider what actions you will need to take to maximise your development during your degree programme. Write these down, they will be used in your PDP later.

▶

SWOT analysis

STRENGTHS	WEAKNESSES
What kind of work experience do I have?	What has held me back in the past?
What qualifications do I have?	Are there gaps in my knowledge, qualifications or experience?
Do I have any areas of specialist knowledge?	In what areas do I lack confidence?
What skills do I have?	Are there any domestic or family circumstances I need to consider?
What are my personal beliefs or values?	Do I have any health problems or personal concerns?
How much support do I have from others?	What are the weak points of my character?
What are my strengths of character?	
OPPORTUNITIES	**THREATS**
Who do I know who could help me progress?	Is my job safe or are there redundancies at work?
Are there opportunities at work/college where I could develop further?	Are there any potential family or financial problems?
Could I ask to work shadow other colleagues?	Will there be any significant changes to my support network?
Can I see a gap in the market?	Are changes in technology in danger of making my knowledge/skills obsolete?
What opportunities exist after my degree?	
Can I get sponsorship or a grant for further development?	

Define yourself through psychometric testing

Psychometric testing is now a common feature of graduate recruitment. It is well worth trying out a range of tests so you are prepared if they are used in a selection process. They may also give you some insight into areas for development in your Personal Development Plan. The two main types of tests used are aptitude, also known as ability, and personality.

Aptitude tests are used to measure suitability for a particular type of job and you may have experienced this type of testing in applying for employment. Common tests include verbal, numerical and diagrammatic reasoning. Tests should be administered under controlled conditions outlined by the British Psychological Society; they are strictly timed and have definite right or wrong answers. Examples of publishers of selection tests include Assessment for

Selection and Employment (ASE) (www.ase-solutions.co.uk) and Saville and Holdsworth (www.shlgroup.com).

Personality tests are intended to gather information about how and why you do things in your own particular way. They are different from aptitude tests in that there are no right or wrong answers: they are designed to look at your style, not ability, and it is important to answer questions accurately and honestly. You may have heard of the test organisations such as The Morrisby Organisation (www.morrisby.co.uk) that are used for careers guidance, or the Myers-Briggs Type Indicator (MBTI) which is frequently used by employers. A shortened version of this can be accessed at www.teamtechnology.co.uk. Another popular instrument is by Meredith Belbin which looks at team roles. Most university careers services run practice test sessions, and there are some useful links on the Prospects website (www.prospects.ac.uk).

ACTIVITY 5 Take an aptitude test

Log onto the UK test publisher Saville and Holdsworth's website at www.shldirect.com and practise some aptitude tests. Look at the feedback you receive. Does this suggest any areas for development? You can also volunteer to take new tests as part of a trial and receive personal feedback.

Analyse your job description and person specification

If you are currently employed in a role which you wish to extend, look carefully at your job description and accompanying person specification. To what extent do you meet the essential and desirable criteria listed? Consider what current skills need to be maintained or improved. Next consider where you lack confidence or have limitations. Could these be areas you need to include in your own development plan? If possible, ask your personnel department for the details of the post at the next level up. Do these give you pointers as to areas you could usefully develop? Even if you are not in a post that you see as part of your future plan, this may still be a useful exercise.

Analyse your transferable skills

Transferable skills are those you possess that can be applied in different situations. Often these are of great interest to your employer as they indicate the innate qualities you will bring to your job. There are several different terms for these; your university may refer to them as key skills, core skills, employability skills, graduate skills, hard and soft skills, personal skills or personal transferable skills. Providing evidence of these can be difficult as they seem rather intangible. A useful way to audit these key skills can be by comparing them to national key skills standards. You could also look at the skills you should be covering in your degree. These will be listed in the appropriate subject benchmarking statement on the QAA website (**www.qaa.ac.uk/academicinfrastructure/benchmark**). There should be details of this in your course handbook.

ACTIVITY 6

Consider the key skills of numeracy (application of number), literacy (communication skills) and information technology (IT). Have a look at the standards produced by the Qualifications and Curriculum Authority (QCA) and map yourself against them (**www.qca.org.uk**). Do you need to develop any of these key skills to progress further? Also look at the level 3 key skill 'Improving Own Learning and Performance': how do you rate against this? Find out if your college offers you an opportunity to be accredited for any of these skills. You will also find a sample portfolio for assessment against these standards on the QCA website.

Drawing up your own Personal Development Plan

A sample Personal Development Plan is produced below; however, you can produce your own plan in whatever format you wish. Remember, personal development does not just happen while you are formally studying, but takes place throughout your life. There are lots of ideas of what you can do after your degree in the final chapter, so it is a good idea to keep your plan on a computer so that it can be regularly updated. If you look on the internet you will find a number of examples of templates which could be used.

When you are setting goals, do try and make sure they are SMART – specific, measurable, agreed upon, realistic and time-based. However, the acronym SMART can be extended to give a broader definition, and it is worth checking that your development plan is:

S – specific, significant, stretching, short
M – measurable, meaningful, motivational
A – agreed upon, attainable, achievable, acceptable, action-oriented
R – realistic, relevant, reasonable, rewarding, results-oriented
T – time-based, timely, tangible, trackable.

Sample Personal Development Plan

Development need	Action	Results expected	Support required to fulfil action	Target dates for completion and review
Clearly describe what you need to learn here.	Detail the specific actions you need to take to meet your need. These could be a mixture of activities: work-based, formal development, informal and self-directed learning, and activities outside work	What will you have learned? This is the measure to show that you have achieved your objectives. It could be a qualification, or NVQ units; being able to put new skills into practice; improved management effectiveness, e.g. meeting all your deadlines.	The costs in time and money. Whose support do you need to turn this plan into reality – a colleague, manager, mentor, employer, friend?	The timescales by which you intend to have achieved this part of your development plan. Be realistic – small successes achieved quickly will provide motivation towards longer-term goals.

Producing a professional development portfolio

Different types of portfolio

For assessment purposes a portfolio might be defined as a structured collection comprising labelled evidence of your learning and critical reflection on it. Yet the situation is complicated, and David Baume (2003) identifies a number of different types of portfolio. You may have already produced a portfolio for a National Vocational Qualification or put together a Record of Achievement (RoA) while you were at school. However, it is important that you are clear about the kind of portfolio you are required to produce for your course.

The portfolio as repository

This is a portfolio at its simplest level: a collection of materials preferably with a structure and an index. This could be as simple as a course file, or kept online with the materials stored digitally. If your portfolio is going to be assessed, it is unlikely that a repository style portfolio will be what is required, although you may need to keep some sort of course file.

The portfolio for development

David Baume describes this type of portfolio as a compost heap, an image which he intends to convey 'not darkness and odour, but rather something that is refined over time, enriched by addition, reduction and turning over' (Baume, 2003:4). In addition to acting as a repository, it can function as your own personal workspace, representing your current state of thinking about your course, collecting materials from a wide range of sources in preparation for production of assignments. This sort of portfolio will be in a constant state of flux, and so needs to be organised and indexed. Again, this is essentially a private portfolio, and unlikely to be appropriate for assessment.

The portfolio for assessment

This form may well make use of the contents of the development portfolio and the repository portfolio, but will extend them by commentary and reflection. Your lecturer will expect to see additional annotation of the contents. This may include reflection on feedback from your academic staff on assessed work, mentors, line managers and peers, to demonstrate how knowledge and understanding have been advanced.

Case Study To start you off, Niki advises that you 'keep anything you think may be useful in a separate box and record all your thoughts in a notebook, no matter how trivial you think they may be'.

ACTIVITY 7 Clarify parameters

Before you begin to compile your assessment portfolio you need to ask your tutor:

- Is there advice on the form, structure, size and content of the portfolio?
- What guidance is there on presentation?
- Is there a maximum word limit for the critical reflection?
- Does there need to be a bibliography?
- Who will see your portfolio? The answer to this question may influence what you want to include.
- What exactly are the required learning outcomes?
- What assessment criteria will be used?
- What opportunities for formative assessment will be provided before the portfolio is due in?
- Whether it is possible to see assessed portfolios from former students?

What to include

Clearly each discipline has its own characteristic forms of working records and products. If you are a scientist you may produce laboratory reports; engineering students may produce design sheets; and social science students, reports and essays. The main requirement for the evidence in your portfolio is that it is appropriate to the field of study. It is possible that little or no evidence will be produced especially for the portfolio. You may be able to gather evidence from your work, during fieldwork or observations, and across all modules of the teaching programme.

What will be written especially for the portfolio is some form of critical reflection or commentary which is supported by this evidence.

ACTIVITY 8 Collect evidence

Think about all the possible evidence you could collect that is relevant to your particular area of study. Then look at the suggestions from Early Years Education students below. All these students are employed in nurseries or similar settings while they are studying for their degree. Are there any items you now want to add to your list, or any you would take issue with?

Early Years Education – possible evidence for professional development portfolio

CV	Analysis against Early Years Practitioner Standards
Person specification for job	Job description
Copies of educational qualifications	Probation/appraisal records
Observations of working with children	Assignments from course modules
Photographs of children's work	Anonymised photographs of the nursery
Witness statements	Anonymised video clips
Staff development plans and records	Feedback from peers and tutors
Copies of e-mails	Minutes of meetings
Evidence of using IT	Staff newsletters
Results of school surveys	References
Letters of commendation	Audio tapes
Thank you notes from teachers and parents	

Collecting the evidence

When you have completed the activity above, you will have started to formulate your ideas about the contents and structure of your portfolio. It is never too early to begin to collect the evidence. Many of our students started by putting documents into a box file, which is fine, but you do need to start sorting it at an early stage. You are not being asked to become filing clerks, but you need to get organised early enough to make the most of the finished portfolio. Remember, selection is more important than collection.

Case Study Cathy suggests that you 'do not put in unnecessary materials – keep it tight'.

Your evidence needs to be:

- valid, this means it demonstrates what you claim it does;
- reliable, that you can consistently do what you claim;
- current, it is something you did recently; ask your tutor to define how far back in time you can go;
- sufficient, this means it is enough to demonstrate what you claim, and finally;
- accurate, it is what actually happened.

It is important that you clearly label your evidence with, as a minimum:

- its title or name, and what the evidence is, if this is not immediately clear;
- the date of production;
- the authors, if you are submitting something produced collaboratively;
- how to access it, if you are producing a portfolio using information technology.

Think about the structure

An explicit structure and signposting through an index are vital, both for you and your tutor. Although you may prefer to be given a template for the structure of your portfolio this is unlikely to happen, as tutors will want to ensure you feel ownership; this includes determining form as well as content. You may find this freedom frustrating, many students do initially. If you would like some further guidance you could consider the following ideas for its organisation:

- by time, on a daily, weekly or monthly basis around a reflective diary and cross-referenced to it;
- around the learning outcomes being demonstrated, with a distinct portfolio section for each learning outcome or assessment criterion to be addressed;
- around underpinning knowledge, professional values, or occupational standards if they exist;
- around evidence from each of the modules on your degree. In this case you could include a representative sample of your work, together with a critical commentary showing what has been learned from any poor performances, and how this learning has been applied to improve;

- mapped against various work tasks you carry out or cross-referenced to your job description;
- around an analysis of the knowledge, skills and attitudes required by the person specification for your post.

Writing a critical commentary

The first part of this chapter has covered writing a reflective journal, and one possible strategy is to cross-reference items of evidence into your journal. However, your assessment may not require a journal, just a portfolio. You should still read the beginning of the chapter because the techniques for writing your critical commentary are the same, but it will not be presented in a diary format.

Remember, assessment will generally be of the critical reflection rather than the evidence itself. The critical reflection is there to make sense of the evidence and to show what you have learned. You should make appropriate referenced use of theoretical sources. This is expected at undergraduate level and is essential at postgraduate level, where you should consider how you apply theoretical or other ideas from the literature to particular topics, either from your work or study.

It is a good idea to show your portfolio to your colleagues and peers. This feedback process is very important, and they may be able to give you some useful advice. It is always helpful to see how other people have structured their portfolio, and to ask them why they have done it in that way.

Creating an e-portfolio

There are many different ways to produce an e-portfolio. There are dedicated e-portfolio software applications such as PebblePad (**www.pebblelearning. co.uk**), Elgg (**http://elgg.net**) and OSP (**www.theospi.org**). A portfolio can take the form of a blog or social networking site (see chapter 4 for more information). You may prefer a visual site like Flickr (**www.flickr.com**) if you wish to put up collections of pictures, or YouTube (**http://uk.youtube.com**) if your work is performance orientated, or you may prefer a written blog like WordPress (**http://wordpress.org**). In all of these cases, clear indexing is particularly important. You should ask for specialist help if you wish to use the university's Virtual Learning Environment (VLE) facilities, such as Blackboard or WebCT, to create and store your portfolio. These systems have considerable possibilities, and increasingly you may be able to store and then transfer your data in standard formats between different institutions.

ACTIVITY 9 Access the web

Explore the following websites and consider how you might use them to develop an e-portfolio:

- Centre for Recording Achievement www.recordingachievement.org/eportfolios
- ePortfolios.ac.uk www.eportfolios.ac.uk
- ePortfolios portal http://danwilton.com/eportfolios
- PebblePad www.pebblelearning.co.uk
- Open Source Portfolio (OSP) www.theospi.org

Checklist for submission of your portfolio

You will find the following checklist helpful before you submit your portfolio for assessment:

- Is it clear and tidy enough so that the assessor can rapidly understand, analyse and assess it? A new lever arch file with clear dividers for each section, an index and numbered pages gives a good impression.
- Does it only contain relevant documentation? Our view is that a portfolio should be no larger than an A4 lever arch file; any more than that and you may not have been sufficiently discriminating about the contents. Bear in mind your tutor will be assessing a larger number of these portfolios – quality not quantity will earn you good marks.
- Have you included only photocopies of relevant qualification certificates or items of personal value? Although staff should make every effort to safeguard your portfolio you need to make sure there is nothing in it that cannot be replaced.
- Do you need to get written permission to use any of the evidence, or should you make any of the evidence anonymous? Particular issues apply when using photographs of children or vulnerable people in a portfolio. Be aware that evidence from work may be of a confidential nature.
- Is the portfolio appropriately presented? The details of presentation of written work in chapter 8 will be helpful here. However, you also need to consider visual presentation. Does your portfolio give the impression you want it to give?

Using your portfolio after you have finished your degree

Portfolios to support presentations for interviews

Increasingly employers tell us they want to see what applicants can do as well as what they know. You can use an edited version of your portfolio at an interview for employment, or further study. This will bring to life your experience, qualifications and learning. It should be a much reduced version of your assessment portfolio, containing only the relevant work of which you are most proud. You should always ask in advance if the employer wishes to see it, and then tailor each presentation portfolio to each interview.

An APEL portfolio

You may be able to collate some of your work into a portfolio to claim APEL (Accreditation of Prior Experiential Learning) against occupational or professional standards. In this case you will need to carefully index your work and provide a commentary and evidence to show that all or some of the particular qualification requirements have been achieved. APEL is a rigorous process and requires reflection, analysis and theoretical underpinning to demonstrate what you have learned from your experiences. If you are going to produce an APEL portfolio you need to clarify the formal requirements of the process and what support is available from your academic institution.

A continuing professional development portfolio

You may also be able to use an amended version of your portfolio to demonstrate continuing professional development for the purposes of registration, membership or licensing of a professional body or you may be able to use it as part of your appraisal scheme at work.

References and further reading

www.ase-solutions.co.uk – the website of Assessment for Selection and Employment.

Baume, D. (2003) *Supporting Portfolio Development*, York: Learning and Teaching Support Network Generic Centre.

Centre for Excellence in Media Practice – www.cemp.ac.uk/research/reflectivelearning is the link for comprehensive information written by Jenny Moon. It is possible to download information from her books on learning journals and reflective practice free of charge from this site providing the source is acknowledged.

Centre for Recording Achievement – www.recordingachievement.org is the website of the Centre for Recording Achievement and supports the implementation of progress files, professional development planning and e-portfolios.

Cottrell, S. (2003) *Skills for Success: the personal development planning handbook*, Basingstoke: Palgrave Macmillan.

Cowan, J. (1998) *On Becoming An Innovative University Teacher: reflection in action*, Buckingham: Society for Research into Higher Education and Open University Press.

http://danwilton.com/eportfolios – an e-portfolios portal.

http://elgg.net – provides e-learning portfolio software.

www.eportfolios.ac.uk – provides advice on developing e-portfolios.

www.flickr.com – a social networking site for presenting e-portfolios visually.

Gray, D., Cundell, S., Hay, D. and O'Neill, J. (2004) *Learning through the Workplace: a guide to work-based learning*, Cheltenham: Nelson Thornes. Chapter 7 by Jean O'Neill contains useful information and advice about portfolio building.

www.learning-styles-online.com – provides an analysis of learning styles.

Megginson, D. and Whitaker, V. (2003) *Continuing Professional Development*, London: Chartered Institute of Personnel and Development.

Moon, J. A. (2006) *Learning Journals: a handbook for academics, students and professional development*, London: Kogan Page.

Moon, J. A. (2004) *A Handbook of Reflective and Experiential Learning*, London: Routledge Falmer.

Moon, J. A. (1999) *Reflection in Learning and Professional Development*, London: Routledge Falmer.

www.morrisby.co.uk – publishes psychometric tests for careers guidance

www.palgrave.com/skillsforstudy/pdp – provides a range of downloadable PDP materials

www.pebblelearning.co.uk – provides PebblePad software for e-portfolios.

www.prospects.ac.uk – provides a wide range of practice tests for graduates.

www.qaa.ac.uk/academicinfrastructure/benchmark – contains subject benchmarking statements.

Quality Assurance Agency (2001) *Guidelines for HE Progress Files,* Gloucester: QAA.

Schön, D. A. (1983) *The Reflective Practitioner*, New York: Basic Books.

www.shldirect.com – the website of Saville and Holdsworth which publish selection tests.

www.teamtechnology.co.uk – publishes Myers-Briggs type indicator tests.

www.theospi.org – the website of the Open Source Portfolio software for e-portfolios.

http://wordpress.org – for written portfolios.

http://uk.youtube.com – social networking site suitable for performance portfolios.

3 Strategies for supporting learning

If you are going to survive the difficulties of managing your workload at the same time as studying successfully, you will need to use every form of assistance that is available to support your learning. Fortunately, higher education establishments are much more aware of the diverse needs of their students than in the past and are therefore more geared up to providing for them, but it is up to you to identify what you need and find out what is available.

It also makes sense for you to find out who you talk to if what you need is either not available, offered at inconvenient times, or is too costly. Universities value what their students tell them and are very often able to effect changes.

This chapter covers:

- using the Learning Resources Centre
- reading effectively
- making notes and effective summaries of texts
- identifying key points from lectures
- learning in tutorials, groups and seminars
- looking at available support for improving basic skills.

Using the Learning Resources Centre

The library in a university or college is most often called the Learning Resources Centre because it contains computing facilities, audio-visual aids and quiet places for you to study, as well as books, journals and other publications. It is one of the most useful ways to support your learning in your university, because all the resources you need are close to hand.

Case Study	Anneca, who has just graduated, says: 'Take advantage of the facilities at the library, read back on seminar notes, study and read alongside lectures. A lot of students only go to the library when they have to do an assignment, but make sure you are reading while studying.'

Showing proficiency in communication, which includes, speaking, listening, reading writing and discussing and finding information, is one of the key skills which all programmes in higher education must include. So, whatever the degree or qualification you are aiming to obtain, these skills will form a fundamental part of your study. Your Learning Resources Centre has a very important part to play in your success if you use it wisely. However, the range and quality of resources can vary enormously in different colleges and universities, so it does make sense to check if your university has arrangements with other institutions that you can also use. The local public library is another source of support which could be very useful for you, especially if you have limited time for travel to your university. In most universities, as soon as you are enrolled onto a course you will be given a student number, and with it automatic access to university facilities. It makes sense for you to discover what the Learning Resources Centre offers as soon as you are able.

What can you usually expect to find?

- books for reference and loan, newspapers, journals and reference sources in print and electronic format
- past exam papers
- slides, videos, DVDs and audio collections
- sound and recording equipment
- video studios, video conferencing and playback facilities
- multimedia production and coursework preparation facilities
- open-access computing suites, offering a range of software, courses and an online learning environment
- archives and special collections
- media services for photocopying, binding, laminating and equipment loan.

Many universities also provide core reading lists at this stage so you can also start to prepare in good time. Even if they have not, it is still worth investigating the Learning Resources Centre so that you are familiar with it when your studies begin. Check what is available: you can do this online first, but it does make sense, once you have checked the hours of opening, to go in person. Most libraries will also organise an induction for you where you can learn how to find what you need.

ACTIVITY 1 Learn about your resources

On your first visit find out:

- if a tour of the Learning Resources Centre is provided and when;
- where the specialist resources you might need are located;
- where the help desks are and who can support your learning;
- where the reference books, such as dictionaries, encyclopaedias and directories, and the journals are located;
- if there is software and media support, and where?
- how the library system works; is it computerised or do they still have a card-index system? How can you access the library catalogue?
- what are the loan arrangements for books and can they be renewed online?

Be prepared to ask for help – modern Learning Resource Centres are large and no two universities organise things in the same way. You can waste a lot of time and get very frustrated. See if they have a printed guide or maps and make notes about what you have found out.

Your Learning Resources Centre is the most valuable tool you have to support your learning and work towards success; sadly, it is frequently undervalued and underused. As a student with demands on your time other than study you know it is a very precious commodity. You will want your visits to be as effective as possible.

Hot Tips Getting the best out of your visits

- Have a clear idea of what it is you want to achieve. You may be preparing in advance for a lecture or seminar discussion, or researching for an essay or assignment. Make a rough plan before you go and identify relevant topics that came up in related lectures and seminars.
- Go with a list of the key words you associate with your topic.
- Decide what you can do in the time available. Do not be too ambitious; it is better to complete a small task than to leave when a task is half-finished and not use the data you have collected.
- Try to find a quiet workspace that suits you and is near the resources you need.
- Be disciplined: avoid sitting and chatting with friends, arrange to meet them later when you can talk about what you have found.
- Make visiting your Learning Resources Centre part of your working habit, use it with respect and show others the same courtesy.

Finding a book

Browsing a small library might help you find something useful, on the other hand in a large Learning Resources Centre, it can be time consuming. The following information should help to make searching much more efficient. If you look along the shelves in the Learning Resources Centre you will see they are arranged by number; this is called the Dewey Decimal Classification system (DDC). This system, the most commonly used in the UK, divides knowledge into ten different broad subject areas, called classes, numbered 000–999. Materials which are too general to belong to a specific group (encyclopaedias, newspapers, magazines and so on) are placed in the 000s.

Dewey Decimal Classification

000 General Knowledge: Internet, Computing, Encyclopaedias, Libraries, Newspapers.
100 Philosophy and Psychology: includes Dying and Death, Ethics, Logic.
200 Religions and Mythology: includes world religions, Greek, Roman and other myths.
300 Social Sciences: includes Sociology, Economics, Law and Education.
400 Languages and Grammar: includes Linguistics, Language, Specific Languages.
500 Maths and Science: includes Physics, Biology, Chemistry, Earth Sciences, Zoology.
600 Medicine and Technology: includes Medicine, Engineering, Arrgriculture, Management.
700 Arts and Recreation: includes Architecture, Arts, Music, Planning.
800 Literature and Rhetoric: includes Literature of Specific Languages.
900 Geography and History: includes Travel, Geneology, Archaeology.

Smaller divisions are used to expand each of the classes.

300 Social Sciences
340 Law
    349. 4 Law of Specific Areas
        349.41 Law of Specific Areas: UK

Each of these can also be expanded using decimals if necessary.

If a large number of books are on the same subject matter and they have the same classification number, three letters are added. These represent the author's surname. Then all the books of the same number are arranged alphabetically according to the author's name. This is helpful if the book that you want is not on the shelf because you may be able to find either other titles by the same author or similar texts by different authors.

The majority of the stock, including journals and audio-visual materials, is catalogued and can be searched for in most Learning Resource Centres using the Online Public Access Catalogue (OPAC). This is a great advantage for students with other commitments as this can be done anywhere you have access to the internet and a membership number; items can also be reserved or renewed using OPAC. Also there are usually OPAC terminals located within the Learning Resources Centre and a guide provided to help you.

The library catalogue is organised in three main ways:

- by subject in alphabetical order;
- by author name also in alphabetical order;
- or by the classified number.

ACTIVITY 2 Find a book

Identify a book from the reading list provided by your course and using the information above, see if you can find it. Take a careful note of the classification number and those of the areas you are studying; it will save you time in future. Now look at others in the same classification; will some of them be useful?

If your Learning Resource Centre does not have the text you require you could check other libraries that your university has an agreement with. Your university may also be part of the Society of College, National and University Libraries (SCONUL) access scheme whereby you will be granted the same borrowing rights that you enjoy in your university LRC at any of the participating higher education libraries in the UK and Ireland. You will need to be prepared to show proof of your membership of your current LRC; your library card is usually sufficient. Check what is required before you go as your own LRC's policy may be different. You could also make use of the Inter Library Loan system. Check who is responsible and make your request. Remember they will need as much detail as possible to help them, so provide the author(s) name(s), date of publication, title of book and country of origin and publisher. There is usually a charge for this service, but you may be permitted a few free requests (do check as it can be quite an expensive service).

ACTIVITY 3 Check SCONUL

Check the following website to see whether you can benefit from the SCONUL agreement www.access.sconul.ac.uk/members.

Using journals and newspapers

Most Learning Resource Centres will have past and present copies of a range of journals and newspapers. Some of these will be hard copy, but for obvious reasons, more and more are now provided electronically. It is worth browsing the titles to see if there are any that might support your studies; have a quick look at the articles. Each has an abstract which is a summary of its contents; a quick look at some of the abstracts will tell you if the journal will be useful to you. It is not a good idea to decide on the basis of the title alone as they can sometimes be misleading or even off-putting. You are usually able to photo-copy useful articles but check the copyright restrictions; usually you will only be allowed one article or up to ten per cent of a journal.

Looking at journals online is easier if you have already identified useful ones. There are thousands to choose from and browsing will take too much time. If you look through the reading lists you were given you will find that some of the references are from journals. Clearly, these will be worth investigating when you are trying to find information for your studies. More about this can be found in the following chapter.

For those of you in work, it is worthwhile checking whether your workplace receives journals or trade publications that might be useful. They may even have related texts which they might be prepared to lend.

ACTIVITY 4 Identify useful journals

List the names of journals you have already found that are going to be useful for you. Keep the list in a handy place, and on your PC as well, so that you can add others as you find them. Make a note of where you found them so that time is not wasted trying to find things again.

Using the internet and electronic sources

More and more students are beginning to rely on the internet to support their studies; especially those with heavy additional commitments such as work or family, when working from home is often essential. However, it is important to ask yourself: 'What is going to be the most efficient method to find out what I can do to support my learning?' Many times the answer will be the internet, but not every time. Let us think about alternatives:

- dictionaries, specific directories and up-to-date encyclopaedias are often easier to access and quicker to use than the internet;
- the authenticity and accuracy of books is checked through the process of editing and reviewing; the internet comes with no guarantee;
- books can be read in your own time, while you are travelling, between lectures or when you have short periods of useful time. Additionally, you may not always have access to the internet;

- your course tutors provide reading lists; some are long to allow you to select; others are short and it will be usual for you to have read all or most that are recommended. You will need to find out what is expected.

Reading effectively

Hints to help identify and select useful information

Now that you know how to find information in the Learning Resources Centre, how can you find texts that are useful without reading the whole book to help you decide? You could read the whole text, but as a general rule it is unwise to at this stage unless:

- it is too good to put down;
- it is a set text;
- it comes highly recommended by someone whose opinion you value; or
- it is the only one you have found.

Otherwise it makes sense to use other strategies to select texts:

- Is the book one of the key texts recommended to you?
- Has the author or editor been recommended in your book list?
- Is the publication recent or the most up-to-date in the field of your study? You can usually find the date that the book was printed on the reverse side of the title page.
- Read the publisher's 'blurb', often situated on the back cover; look for information which is relevant to the essay or assignment.
- Check the bibliography. Is the author/editor citing authors you know are important in your field?
- Are there diagrams, tables, illustrations that seem to be relevant?

Skimming and scanning

Skimming and scanning are ways in which people quickly gain an overview of a written piece without actually reading. When you skim you let your eye wander over the page quickly to pick out key words or phrases, with scanning you are taking in the words quickly to gain an overview. They are useful skills to gain; with practice you will develop your own techniques.

- Scan the contents page(s) as you would look for an entry in a telephone directory; about three times your normal reading speed. Do the headings look like the areas that are relevant to your topic? Are they the right level for you?
- Quickly scan the introduction and conclusion of chapters that seem relevant, or the abstract and conclusion of a journal article. This will tell you whether it is worth reading. For a short piece of work it may be all you need.
- Look up your key words in the index and find the relevant pages; skim the pages or paragraphs to find your words. Does it look useful? If so,

read it more thoroughly. Is the author dealing with the topic in a way that will be useful for you?

■ Keep thinking about the meaning of what you are reading.

■ Mark useful pages with a Post-it flag, if the information you need is contained on a few pages only, photocopy them; but do not forget to photocopy the title page and make a note of the date of publication and publisher. Make a note of the chapter title and page numbers if a different person wrote it. This information will be essential when you write your bibliography.

Activity 5 Skim read

Skim read an article in a journal. Put it to one side and then make notes about what you remember, identifying the key points. Now read the article more slowly, this time noting what information you might have missed. Hopefully, you will be pleasantly surprised.

Activity 6 Speed race

Try the speed reading exercise at this web address: **www.bbc.co.uk/skillswise**, go to 'tutor centre' skills a–z, click 's' for skimming to find exercises

Reading for information

Now you have found some texts which you are sure will be useful, it is time to start real reading. We read in different ways to suit our purpose; reading a novel is completely different from reading the newspaper or finding out what is on at the cinema. How important we think the information is, the writing style of the author, and our familiarity with the topic, will determine the way we read. That is why we are often not very relaxed when we are reading academic texts; yet you will absorb more information if you are not tense. Make sure you are comfortable, you are warm enough, there is not too much distraction and the lighting is right for you. Think creatively about this, lunchtimes at work might be perfect. Research indicates that we absorb less from text onscreen, so if possible it makes sense to print out key information. You will also have it to hand when you want to look at it again and can mark up or identify key points.

Case Study Margaret said: 'I found I absorbed information more in a really quiet atmosphere, sometimes I read aloud to myself.' Emma advises you to 'make notes as you read, don't set yourself too much to do in one go and use Post-it tabs for reference' and Clair said: 'Try reading your books in bed or where you have peace and quiet and if you are not taking it in, stop and try again later.'

Have a dictionary or technical guide to hand or be linked to the internet so that you can quickly identify any words you do not know. It is a good idea to keep a glossary of the new words and their meanings in your notebook. Do not worry if you are slow to start with; you will improve with practice. If a text is difficult, read it once quite quickly, then a second time a little more slowly. If it is very difficult to understand, put it to one side and read another article on a similar topic that is easier to absorb. Make notes about the text; when you return to the harder one you should find it easier because you have already started to associate words and ideas about the topic.

Activity 7 Read and understand

Read an article from a newspaper; time yourself for two minutes. How much did you read? How much did you understand? Repeat this activity with articles of increasing difficulty. Try to get your reading up to about 200 words per minute. Remember it is more important to understand what you read than to read quickly.

Hot Tips Improving your speed

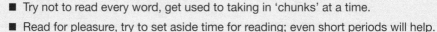
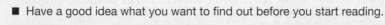

- Have a good idea what you want to find out before you start reading.
- Try not to read every word, get used to taking in 'chunks' at a time.
- Read for pleasure, try to set aside time for reading; even short periods will help.
- Build up a glossary of specific words, ideas and concepts; keep them to hand until you are confident that you understand them completely.
- Try not to read too slowly, it can stop you understanding the meaning; better to read something twice quickly.
- Start with easy texts; tackle the difficult ones once you are familiar with the topic.
- Make notes about what you have read, share your ideas with a partner or mark up a text (only photocopies please) as soon as you can after reading it.
- Create your own table of contents when you are reviewing material.

Research at the University of Wolverhampton has found that most of their undergraduate students gained the majority of their information through lectures and found effective reading to supplement and reinforce their learning difficult (Clarke, 2007). The researcher concluded this was a problem because there is a clear link between efficient reading, critical thinking and appropriate levels of academic writing (Wyse, 2006). These skills are not only essential for academic success but also for the world of employment.

What kind of reader are you?

Surface readers read the text to gather facts and information for a task. They are often unaware of the way in which they are reading. Deep readers try to identify what the author's viewpoint is; they will explore the logic of what they are reading, question its authenticity, and identify assumptions that are unsupported. They are expanding their knowledge and relating what they read to their own experiences and previous learning. Deep reading is commonly referred to as critical reading.

Activity 8 Are you a critical reader?

Ask yourself the following questions:

- Can you identify what the main theme is and what the author is focusing on?
- Can you identify what the key arguments or issues are and what has been left out?
- Do you check to see if there is evidence to support claims?
- Do you check to see if a contemporary issue or philosophy has influenced the author?
- Do you check the viewpoint of the author?
- Do you check who the text is written for (other academics, students, members of the public)?
- Do you know how the author's argument compares with other material on the topic?
- Do you notice if there is bias in the way the evidence is presented?
- Can you identify the type of writing style the author is using?

If you can honestly answer 'yes' to most or all of these questions, you are a critical reader. If not, look at the questions to help you become one.

Case Study	Lynda says: 'Re-read information and read the recommended books, little and often, rather than having loads to read when assignments are due.'

Making notes and effective summaries of texts

Making effective notes is an essential part of reading; it will increase your reading speed and is an essential resource for essays or assignments. Try to evaluate the relevance of what you are reading; the information may be useful for something you are working on at the time or you may realise that it has the potential for later use. Either way it makes sense to make it possible to use again later by making notes.

> **Case Study**
>
> LisaMarie states: 'I would recommend students make notes about what they find important, noting key words to trigger their memories.'

The way we make notes and store information is an individual preference, but having a system is essential. Students with other commitments will find that developing effective note-making skills can make a fundamental difference to their success. Everybody makes notes in their own way; after all, they are for you so it is important that they suit your purpose. The notes may be neat or messy; it really does not matter so long as you can make use of them. Try not to cram too many words on one page; white space helps the eyes to focus on the words and also allows for later additions if necessary. Experienced and successful students will tell you that one of the first and most important things they learned was how to make effective notes and how to store them for easy retrieval. They will also tell you cautionary tales about the hours wasted looking for badly stored references and texts.

> **Case Study**
>
> Sally says: 'Try and retain some sort of order for each assignment and keep all the papers for each assignment separate; it is easy to get things mixed up and the wrong notes can be a headache to try to sort out.'

Always start by dating your notes and including bibliographic details: author/editor name(s), initials, title, date, publisher and place of publication. Remember to include page numbers, journal title, volume and issue number for journals and articles. If you are preparing for an essay or assignment, it makes sense to put these details into your computer as well, so that you build your bibliography from the start, or you can use a specialist package such as EndNote. Number your pages and put a brief title on each so that you keep them together. To begin, you may keep all your notes in one folder using dividers to separate the topics. Later as you gather more they will probably need keeping in different files.

There are a number of different forms of note-making; familiarise yourself with all the strategies so that you can select the one most suited to the task you have at the time. Whatever system you use, make sure it is organised and easy to access. Try to simplify your writing by using abbreviations. Work out a system you will remember and keep a key nearby until you are familiar with the ones you use. Additionally, make sure your note making is thorough; it is a waste of time rewriting them, it is better to go over them and add in further thoughts.

Before you start, be clear about why you are making the notes. There is a temptation, particularly when you are inexperienced, to copy great chunks of text. This is not only time wasting, but is not helpful and could lead you to unintentional plagiarism. There is more about this topic in chapter 7. However, you might, whilst reading, find some parts of the text which you want to quote. Copy it out carefully and make sure you identify it in your notes as a quotation, recording the page number. You could also use a particular colour highlighter in your notes to denote potential quotes.

Reasons for making notes

- to enable you to understand the forthcoming lecture;
- to enable you to consolidate your learning from a previous lecture;
- to help you clarify your understanding of a text;
- to prepare for a set topic or assignment;
- to identify a potential topic for investigation;
- to compare different views on a topic.

Techniques for note-making

Notes on handouts or texts

This method can only be used if you own the text. Although it is useful to make notes on the text while you are skimming and scanning as a first stage, these notes are only useful for a short while. They are quite difficult to read later on and you will probably have to read the whole text again.

Headings and bullet points

This is a very common method of note-making and is particularly useful if you are working straight on to the computer. The heading refers to the subject matter of the text, with all the key points identified and bulleted. Because it is quite difficult to learn how to do this at first, try reading each paragraph and identifying the key point it is making. This is usually identified at the beginning of the paragraph and then expanded, with the last sentence bringing the paragraph to a conclusion. This technique does make you think very carefully about what you are reading and is dependent on a systematic structure in the text.

Double notes

With the page divided into two, use the first column to identify the key points and summarise what you are reading. The second column is your commentary on the notes. This is useful for separating your ideas from those in the text.

Concept maps or 'sprays'

If you find it easier to take in information from visual display this may be a good method for you. The key point, topic or question is placed in the middle of the page. Lines are drawn from the centre with each of the main topic areas or themes written on them. Each line leads you into greater depth about the topic by subdividing each time another related point is identified.

Concept maps can allow you to summarise many pages of reading and help you to concentrate on identifying the themes. For ease of understanding they can also be colour coded to represent different themes or topics. They can be stimulating because they are so visual, but they can be too super-ficial for complex ideas or personal reflection.

Grids, tables, flowcharts and timelines

Some information readily lends itself to being recorded as a grid. For exam-ple, the theories of intelligence held by different writers could be subdivided into sections, one for each of the writers matched against a second column identifying their theory.

If you wanted to record this information in greater detail you might use a table where you identify the types of intelligence, the names of the theorists, a summary of their key points and your analytical comments. Recording information this way enables you to cross-tabulate and makes analysis and comparison easier. Again it can be too superficial. Flowcharts and timelines are an excellent way of recording a linear process, a sequential argument or historical events and are often found in textbooks for science disciplines, engineering, psychology and education.

Linear notes

This method involves identifying the key points and ideas. Using your own style it can be easy to revise from and allows for in-depth analysis. You can use arrows and dotted lines to link points, boxes, underlining or other visual markers to make important points stand out. Highlighters or a different coloured pen can also be used.

Case Study Eric said: 'At school I did not enjoy making notes. I realise now that I preferred learning visually so now I use bright colours and pictures to help. Use coloured pens and spider diagrams.'

Coping with unfamiliar words and complex sentences

When you are reading texts it is not unusual to come across words you do not understand and sentences which are so long that you lose the meaning by the time you get to the end of it. Having a dictionary to hand can help if the word is not known to you but is in everyday use. However, the word may represent a particular concept or idea, appropriate in a specialist context. In this case the dictionary definition will be confusing. A specialist dictionary might help, but the author may be using the word in a way which has not been defined. This is particularly the case in social science literature where the meaning of words is frequently contested. Another approach is to look for clues in the text. Making a note of the difficult word and then reading on often gives sound clues as to the possible meaning. Even though it may not give you a precise meaning of the word, it allows you to move on in the reading and gain understanding of the text.

Some authors are prone to writing in very long sentences. If you find a sentence which is difficult to understand because of its length, try breaking it up into smaller, simpler statements. This may help you to understand its meaning. If you have found it difficult it is quite likely that others have as well. If it does not help, you could study the sentences before and after it to see what clues they give. The key is to take your time and be active about finding the solution, not to get into a panic and let it get in the way of your learning.

Identifying key points from lectures

Listening is one of the most important skills we have. How well we listen has a major impact on our effectiveness as students or employees and on our relationships with others.

- We listen to obtain information.
- We listen to understand.
- We listen to learn.

Given the amount of listening we do, you would think we would be quite skilled at it, but we are not. Depending on which research you read (Petrass, 1999; Goby and Lewis, 2000) it is claimed that we only remember between 25 and 50 per cent of what we hear. Improving your listening skills is going to be an excellent way to support your learning.

Hot Tips **Effective listening**

- Look directly at the speaker.
- Concentrate on their words.
- Do not allow distracting thoughts.

- Try not to be preparing a reply or response.
- Avoid being distracted by environmental factors.
- 'Listen' to the speaker's body language.
- Avoid side conversations.

It takes a lot of concentration and determination to be an active listener.

Case Study Clair advises: 'During a lecture things can move very fast. If there is ever anything that you don't understand then put your hand up and ask. The likelihood is that there are others in the same boat as you, they don't understand and are afraid to ask.'

Making notes

Making notes in lectures is not only a useful way of helping you to remember what has been said, it gives you visual information for your revision as well. It also assists your concentration.

Case Study Emma advises that you 'make your own notes on lecture handouts when possible. It means you have the salient point and your own observations together so makes re-reading much more meaningful', and Paula suggests that you 'read your notes after the lecture and again before your next college session'.

Most courses have module handbooks and session notes and handouts. These are usually available in electronic form as part of your Virtual Learning Environment. It makes sense to check these in advance of the lecture if possible. There is a temptation to think that the notes provided will be sufficient to remind you about the lecture later. Although you will not need to write everything down, making further notes on the handouts will help you clarify and understand what has been said. There will be times when handouts are not provided, are not of the quality to assist you later on, or the lecture is delivered without any visual images or texts to help.

The following key points should help you take notes from any lecture or talk:

- Record the date, title of the lecture and lecturer's name on each page.
- Listen carefully to the introduction; this is usually where the key themes are identified; make a note of them.
- Recognise the way points are raised; listen for 'signal' words such as 'first', 'secondly', 'most importantly', 'in addition', 'either', 'or', 'on the one hand', 'on the other hand', 'for example'.
- Summarise what is being said in your own words; most often key points are repeated in slightly different ways.

- If you are having difficulty keeping up you are probably writing too much, try to simplify what you are writing.
- If you miss a point, identify the space and check the handouts or check with a colleague and fill it in.
- Listen carefully to the summary; the lecturer will go over the key points and this should help you fill in any missing information and organise your notes.

Recording the lecture as an alternative

It is perfectly acceptable to ask the lecturer if you may record their lecture. You will have to give assurances that the recording is for your use only as they may be uneasy about you respecting their intellectual property rights. In other words, they may be concerned about you using their work inappropriately. They may legitimately have a concern that you could use an unguarded comment as evidence against them. However, for students with specific difficulties or impairments this may be the only or preferred option. If this method is to be used, checking the quality of the equipment is vital before embarking on purchase. Many recorders will not provide a recording of sufficient quality playback. Recording should never be seen as the 'easy option'; transcription takes an expert twice as long as the recording and you will find that you still have to turn the recording into usable notes.

Storing your notes

There are a variety of ways in which you could store your notes. It is for you to decide what will be most efficient.

> **Case Study** Niki admits to having 'a bit of a rocky start and lots of carrier bags, then I progressed to separate file boxes for each module'.

The following are some suggestions for organising notes:

- **Loose-leaf folder:** Easy to subdivide and to add sections to at a later date.
- **Box files:** Can keep large amounts tidy.
- **Cardboard or plastic folders:** Can be reused and are good for pamphlets and cuttings.
- **Filing cards:** Ideal for brief references, or bibliographies.
- **Notebook:** Easy to carry and pages do not fall out.
- **Concertina file:** Subdivisions already made.
- **Computer:** Easy to edit and use the material.
- **Tape recorder:** Useful for recording speech and good if you prefer to say things rather than write them down.

Whatever you decide you will also need to organise your notes in such a way that you can find them again.

> **Case Study** Sally said this worked for her: 'Make sure you date each page of lecture notes, research papers, handouts, etc. If you have access to a photocopier make sure you take a copy; at least make a note of which book, publisher, etc and what website you visited and the date (for the bibliography). I invested in some Post-it coloured sticky arrows which I found invaluable when marking pages for research and reference.'

You could classify your notes as follows:

- **By date:** This may be useful for a series of lectures which are stored under one heading.
- **Alphabetically:** This is simple to manage.
- **By topic:** This is often the best method as you can add to it as you go along. Choose topics that are easy to file under and that you will remember. They may be the names of the modules or sessions.
- **A mixture of methods:** For example, in date order under a topic heading.

> **Case Study** Patrick says: 'No university course is 'paper-free'. Get yourself some good lever arch files and loads of plastic A4 pockets. Divide your circulated lecture notes, study notes, research into the pockets. Take the relevant ones to lectures. It will reduce your search for notes at revision time enormously. Daily put away your files and pockets.'

Learning in seminars, tutorials and groups

Most universities use a model which intersperses key lectures with group work and seminars. Others may allocate students to a personal tutor who may not be an authority on the subject matter of the module. They will conduct tutorials on more general issues. Tutorials are also provided for one-to-one discussions about work in progress.

Seminars, tutorials and groups are usually much smaller than lectures to encourage student interaction and participation. Some are provided as a means for students to consolidate their learning from the related lecture, others are to extend learning or to allow students to demonstrate their understanding. All should be prepared for.

How to be prepared and get the most from seminars, tutorials and group work

Seminars

Know in advance what the topic of discussion will be. This will most often be found in the module handbook or may be announced at the full lecture. Alternatively, you may have been given a specific topic to prepare for.

- Have annotated notes or handouts from the lecture ready.
- Have notes from your reading of at least one of the recommended texts to hand.
- Be aware of the topicality of your lecture, there may well be information or discussion in the media which you could usefully contribute.
- Do not take criticism of your ideas personally.

In some seminars or discussion groups the tutor uses the time to ensure understanding and will go over the key points of the lecture with you. They will expect you all to contribute what you know and understand. Others will expect you to use the knowledge you have gained from the previous lecture to discuss a topic based on it. Again, you will all be expected to contribute and the lecturer will be noting the quality of your understanding. Either method is essential for you as it helps to consolidate your learning, so do not be tempted to consider it unnecessary. It is also a good opportunity to identify any difficulties you are experiencing and will help to prepare you for the assignment or examination you will undertake.

Tutorials

There are two types of tutorial. Those most common in the arts, social sciences and law will discuss a preset topic. Some are one-to-one, others may be in small groups. The second type is more common in scientific, numerical and engineering type subjects where students will be working on problems or tasks related to the lectures. Tutorials must be prepared for; you are privileged to be given part of your tutor's precious time; it makes sense to use the expertise available.

- Make sure you know what is to be discussed.
- Read in advance.
- Organise your notes so you are able to identify what you have done so far and what you would like advice on.
- If the tutorial has been organised at your request, it is for you to negotiate its nature beforehand so that your tutor can be prepared.
- If you are working on a problem or task it may make sense to prepare for the tutorial with others from your group.
- Relate the topic to the wider issues of the course structure.
- Identify any difficulties or issues.
- Consider all the options.

Group work

Depending on the qualification you are working towards group work will often form part of the formal assessment or learning process. You may be allocated a group or allowed to select one in order to prepare a presentation, lead part of a lecture, or complete a task. Your success will be judged not only on the quality of task completion but also on your ability to work as a team, allowing the individuals to develop within it. However, you all need to work together, putting aside the competitiveness which can develop as a by-product of trying to get high marks. The very act of having to talk about your ideas and support your argument is the best way to really understand something.

Group work is also an invaluable aid to support your learning because as you work together you can:

- discuss issues;
- share points of view and improve understanding;
- clarify any misconceptions;
- generate new ideas;
- re-energise your motivation for study;
- unblock problems or misunderstandings which are getting in the way of learning.

Case Study Patrick said: 'Read up your notes from your library research, highlight any useful arguments. Read your lecture notes for the next day if they are posted on the Virtual Campus.'

Looking at available support for improving basic skills

This book gives you a lot of information and strategies to help you cope with the rigours of academic life. However, most students will want to support their learning by ensuring that their basic skills are sufficiently developed for successful study. Although you have convinced those who have offered you a place on your chosen course that you are capable of achieving a positive outcome, they will have made an assumption that you will take every opportunity to continue to improve.

Although you may have been encouraged whilst still in full-time schooling or at work to identify your learning needs, it requires a considerable mind shift to recognise that once you are in post-compulsory education you are expected to think for yourself. Initially, it is you who identifies your training and support needs and is proactive in finding what is available.

The internet is a valuable source of self-help sites. The following chapter will give you some useful guidance in finding reliable sites and gauging their value, and you will probably want to explore some for yourself. These can be found in the references and further reading section.

Your programme of study may also provide sessions or courses which you can attend, at no cost, to improve the skills you have identified as needing attention. Again, it is your responsibility to find out what is available. Your personal tutor, head of year or course administrator should be able to help. They may also be able to let you know of other support available to you.

It is also worthwhile checking your local authority website to see what they are offering. Many local authorities provide basic skills courses free of charge which may be more convenient for you to attend. Though bear in mind that they will not be specific to your studies and may be of a general nature.

In this chapter we have looked at the range of support which is available to help you succeed in your studies. It is up to you to decide what you need and how to use this assistance.

References and further reading

www.bbc.co.uk/learning/basic_skills.shtml – an excellent BBC site offers online learning addressing a range of skills at different levels. Also quick links to research and development and national test examples.

www.bbc.co.uk/skillswise – another BBC site which aims to enable adults to improve their basic reading, writing and number skills. Learning is offered at different levels with worksheets, quizzes and so on.

Clarke, K. (2007) *Institute for Learning Enhancement, Learning and Teaching Projects 2006–2007,* Wolverhampton University.

www.education.ex.ac.uk/dll/studyskills/note_taking_skills.htm – hints for taking notes from lectures.

Goby, V. P. and Lewis, J. H. (2000) 'The Key Role of Listening in Business: a study of the Singapore insurance industry', *Business Communication Quarterly*, 63 (2) 41–51.

www.keyskillssupport.net/ – Tests to check your level of literacy.

http://openlearn.open.ac.uk/study – skills offers some really useful hints to help you take notes.

Petrass, M. (1999) *Effective Listening Skills: an examination of what skills make for a good listener*, London: Museums, Libraries and Archives Council.

Rowntree, D. (1976) *Learn to Study* (2nd Edition), London: Macdonald and Co. For author's SQ3R approach to note-taking from readings.

www.support4learning.org.uk/ – more help to improve your basic skills. This site can be difficult to access at times.

Wyse, D. (2006) *The Good Writing Guide for Education Students*. London: Sage Publishing.

4 Using technology to enhance your learning

Today most employers will expect you to have skills in using information and communications technology (ICT) and you may feel confident in your ability to use technology at work and at home. This chapter will help you to develop these skills specifically to support your programme of study. You may find that much information returned by search engines is not quality assured or at an appropriate level for university courses, so we will direct you to the best places to look for high-quality, subject-specific information. If you have ever lost or deleted an important file at work or at home, then you will realise that file management is an important skill. We will give you tips on how to keep your computer secure against viruses and other malware (malicious software). Using a Virtual Learning Environment (VLE) for the first time may seem challenging, but it can bring part-time and distance learners together, thus reducing the feelings of isolation you may have if you are not studying full-time. We will look at the best way to use tools such as discussion boards, blogs, wikis and podcasting in your study, and finally we will give some ideas to further develop your ICT skills and gain accreditation for them.

This chapter covers:

- using the internet and electronic resources
- the importance of anti-virus software and backups
- learning online in the virtual classroom
- developing your information technology skills.

Using the internet and electronic resources

The World Wide Web (**www**) is increasingly part of our everyday lives, affecting us at work, at home and when we study. Sometimes people use the terms 'internet' and 'world wide web' interchangeably, but they do refer to two different things. The internet is about the interconnection of computer networks across the world; accessing the web is just one way of using the internet, just as sending an e-mail is another. The web lets you browse pages with text, pictures and sound and so be a useful source of information for work and study. It is quite unlike library catalogues and databases in that it is not so neatly organised, and the information varies greatly in its quality and usefulness. Everyone thinks they know how to search the internet, so why is it sometimes so difficult for us to find the right information? The following sections will help you with this, but if you need to recap on the basics then log on to the BBC's Webwise, a free online learning course on **www.bbc.co.uk/webwise**.

Finding the right search tool

Search engines

When you are using a search engine you are using a tool which searches millions (if not billions) of websites on every subject imaginable. Search engines are handy if you want to find a specific piece of information. 'Google' (**www.google.com**) is the largest search engine and searches many other websites including other types of web documents. These include blog posts, wiki pages, group discussion threads and document formats such as PDFs, Word or Excel® documents and PowerPoint® presentations. However, because not all the web is searchable in Google, it is worth trying the other major search engines such as Ask.com (**www.ask.com**) and Yahoo! Search (search.yahoo.com) to get a second opinion. Meta-search engines use several search engines to come up with a result although, with the exception of Dogpile, they tend to return results for smaller search engines. Try KartOO (**www.kartoo.com**), Dogpile (**www.dogpile.com**) and Clusty (**http://clusty.com**).

ACTIVITY 1 Using different search engines

Key in a specific phrase, to do with your area of study, into each of the search engines and meta-search engines above and skim through the results. Notice the different ways they are displayed.

Subject gateways

These are also called subject guides, subject directories and subject portals. In general these are the best starting points for exploring what is available on the internet to support academic work. Subject gates are trustworthy, too: they are tools, often built by experts from universities and colleges, to enable you to browse good-quality lists of subject resources.

ACTIVITY 2 Log onto these multi-subject gateways and search using your own area of study

Bulletin Board for Libraries (BUBL)	**http://bubl.ac.uk**
Google Scholar	**http://scholar.google.co.uk/**
Intute	**www.intute.ac.uk**

Planning your search strategy

Before you can conduct an effective search for information, you need to be very sure about what it is you are looking for. In other words, you need to focus your query. Try to:

- Use very specific key words or phrases. Be precise and cut out any words that are vague or ambiguous.
- Think about which types of information would be most useful (statistics, news, theories), and search appropriate sources.
- Formulate specific questions that you would like the information to answer or address and write these out in full in the search box. Omit common words like 'the' and 'of'. Do not forget to add any date or geographical limitation to your search.

Hot Tips **Conducting searches**

- Check your spelling.
- Use words that are similar, synonyms, or different spellings.
- If your strategy is still not working try using a different phrase; try another directory or search engine, no two search engines are the same.
- Try the option available on some search engines such as AltaVista or Google to find similar or related documents to one of your relevant hits.
- Use what are known as the Boolean operators – AND, NOT, OR. Using these will find titles which contain all the words you have typed. For example human AND resource AND management will find items containing all three words. Using NOT will help to reduce hits if you have too many. Alternatively you can use plus (+) and minus (-) symbols. The operator OR can also widen your search.

▶

■ Putting double quotes ". . ." at the beginning and ending of a phrase limits the search, "human resource management" will only find items which contain the whole phrase.

Judging the quality of the information

There is so much information on the internet. This means that a lot of what is available is not relevant for you and may not be of the high quality you hope for. It is important that you critically appraise the internet and other resources to decide whether the information they offer is appropriate for your particular purpose. In doing this you should consider its relevance, provenance and reliability and whether it is current.

It is essential to reference any data you use from the internet, although there are sometimes difficulties with the citation of web sources as sites can change or disappear. You will learn how to reference websites correctly in chapter 7, but in the meantime always make a note of the author, title, URL and date of your most recent visit to any website you intend to use. It might be a good idea to 'bookmark' the site if you think it may be useful for future reference.

It is important to deal with relevance first, because even if the information is of high quality, if it is not relevant you should not use it. This will depend much on the context of your query but also on the level at which you are studying. Is the information too specialised or too simple? Now let us turn to the other criteria.

Provenance – who is providing the information and how reliable are they?

As we know, anyone can set up a website, so you should find out who has written the information, and who has published it. You need to decide if they are trustworthy, or are they trying to persuade you, sell you something, inform or misinform you? You can get some clues by looking for:

■ the author's name
■ the organisation publishing the information
■ the contact information
■ the 'about us' pages
■ the URL (Uniform Resource Locator), the website's unique address on the internet.

You need to consider the following:

■ The site may be provided by an official organisation, or an author who might list qualifications. You can check these if you do not recognise them. But be careful, organisations sometimes sell webpage space and they may have little control over the content.

- Look for an overview or introduction, is a position being taken on the issue? You may be able to judge objectivity from the quality of the writing, is it balanced or more emotive?
- Take care with Wikipedia (**www.wikipedia.org**), an online free content encyclopaedia that anyone can edit. Articles here may score highly on relevance but can be less than objective, depending on the source of the information. Tutors differ in their views of Wikipedia; it is best to ask before using this.

Case Study Karen, who is in the first year of her degree, states: 'When researching on the internet for useful references, we were not informed not to use Wikipedia – until after submitting our assignments. A useful list of reliable internet sites before starting our assignments would have benefited us all.'

- Commercial companies want to sell products or services, it will be unlikely that you will get unbiased information.
- Government departments and other political organisations may also favour information that promotes their political aims and influences public opinion or behaviour.

Timeliness – when was the information written?

We assume the web is up to date, but there may be a time delay in updating or adding information. Some information is out of date; some sites have just been abandoned; some sites change or disappear without warning. Reliable sites usually tell you when they were updated.

Ask yourself:

- When was the information originally produced? With peer-reviewed journal articles, the date of publication may not reflect when the information was produced, because it can take time for research to be reviewed.
- Is it still being stored in its original form? This is important for historical documents.
- Has it been updated? Regularly produced reports and statistics mean you may not be looking at the latest edition, check the version you are using is the most recent and that you know when it is likely to be updated.

ACTIVITY 3 Explore the Internet

Log on to the internet and visit the following websites. Think about how you might use them in your study or at work.

BBC News	http://news.bbc.co.uk
The British Library	www.bl.uk

Intute	www.intute.ac.uk
National Statistics Online	www.statistics.gov.uk
UK government reports	www.open.gov.uk

Organising information using social bookmarks

If you use the internet at home or at work you will probably already be using the 'bookmarks' or 'favourites' feature on your browser to store the websites you visit regularly, and perhaps organising topics into sub-folders. However, you will need to set these up on each PC you use unless you use an online social bookmarking tool which can be accessed from any PC connected to the internet. In addition, you can add keyword tags to the sites you save, so you can group together items on the same subject. You can also share your sites with your study group and get recommendations from others.

ACTIVITY 4 Set up an account

Log on to **http://del.icio.us**, set up an account and import your favourites into it. See if other people who have tagged your sites have collected other sites that could be relevant to you.

Downloadable articles and books

As you have seen, many organisations and government sites on the internet offer access to texts such as journals, newspaper articles, conference papers, study tips and so on. But there is considerable variation in what they offer:

- Some are published in print, others are only on the web.
- Some can be downloaded for free.
- Some you can access as read-only text (this cannot be printed).
- Some are in PDF (portable document format) which does not permit changes to the text.
- Some are databases where you can only see the title and an abstract, and you have to take out a subscription to read the article.

Databases are searchable collections of references. There are two main types, bibliographic, which contain references to articles and sometimes an abstract, and full text, which contains the content of the article. They have the advantage of being a very quick means of accessing references to academic material. The information is likely to be of high quality as it has gone through some selection or reviewing process to be included in an academic journal.

In addition, your Learning Resources Centre (LRC) is likely to subscribe to e-Book collections and reference works, sometimes called the 'invisible web' because they are not available on the www. How easily you can download texts will depend on what your LRC subscribes to. For some you need a username and password, as with an Athens account. This is an access management system which provides users with a single sign on to numerous websites. Others you may only be able to access through your Learning Resource Centre's intranet and will need your student ID. A few provide open access to all. Your LRC staff will be trained to help with searching and, in our experience, welcome being contacted by e-mail, telephone or in person for advice.

ACTIVITY 5 Clarify access to resources

You should have received an introduction to the range of online journals and e-books your Learning Resources Centre subscribes to during your induction. If you have not received this, or have doubts about how to use these resources, then ask for help and details of an Athens address and password so you can access these materials at work and at home.

The importance of anti-virus software and backups

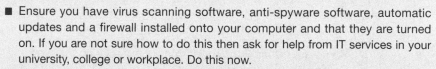

Hot Tips **Safeguard your computer against malware**

The most common malicious software (malware) is in the form of viruses, worms and Trojans, although spyware and adware may also affect your personal data.

- Ensure you have virus scanning software, anti-spyware software, automatic updates and a firewall installed onto your computer and that they are turned on. If you are not sure how to do this then ask for help from IT services in your university, college or workplace. Do this now.

- Do not download or install software from any unknown source; if the software is free and can be downloaded from the internet it will often contain adware or spyware.

- Always virus scan removable data storage devices (such as floppy disks, CDs, flash drives) if they have been used on other computers.

- Viruses are most easily spread by attachments in e-mail messages. If you are unsure about the source of an e-mail attachment, save it to your hard disk and then scan it before opening. Do not open attachments you are not expecting.

Backing up your pc

In addition to saving your work frequently, using the manual and auto save functions, you should make multiple copies of your important data files as a precaution against the original being corrupted or destroyed. This is essential;

hard disks fail, systems crash and, if you are not careful, viruses can infect your files. Always make sure important work for submission is backed up and is kept in more than one location. There are various options in addition to your hard disk at home or at work:

- Assured storage: storing your data on your work or university server either in a shared area or personal work area. Again, if you are not sure how to access this then speak to IT services staff at work or your HE institution.
- CD-ROM: you need to be aware of the difference between CD-R and CD-RW disks. CD-R (read-only) disks are ideal for permanent storage or archiving of information, but the information stored on them cannot be changed. CD-RW (read/writable) disks allow you to add and amend storage information. For both you will need access to a CD writer/driver or CD burner.
- A USB flash drive: or pen drive, is a simple solution for backing up and transporting files as it just plugs into the USB port of the computer. Many fit onto a key ring so they are easy to transport, but also easily lost or stolen. Data can also be corrupted if you do not use the correct procedure to withdraw a flash drive from your pc.

Learning online in the virtual classroom

What is a Virtual Learning Environment (VLE)?

This is an integrated environment of all the online tools you will need for studying, and may include course information, online resources, e-mail and discussion boards, blogs, wikis, podcasts, instant messaging and video conferencing. You may be able to submit your work for final assessment over the VLE and you will usually find your tutor will give you feedback on your ongoing work through the VLE. There are a number of commercial systems such as WebCT and Blackboard although many universities are now swapping to Moodle. Moodle (**www.moodle.org**) is an open source VLE which, unlike standard VLE systems, means that it can be constantly refined by its community of users. This part of the chapter cannot show you how to use your specific VLE – you need to find this out at induction, as all systems vary – but it will give some advice on how to make the best use of various components so you can interact and work collaboratively with others.

If your university or college uses a VLE then you will need to be able to do the following tasks, so check they are covered in any training:

- Activate your university account using your enrolment number.
- Log in to the VLE using a username and password.
- Navigate around the system.
- Access and enrol on your own modules.
- Look at the range of online resources available.
- Know where to go for help and support.

Podcasting

The term 'podcast' is derived from the words iPod and broadcast, and refers to a sequence of digital audio files which can be downloaded from the internet, transferred to a mobile device, such as an iPod or MP3 player, and listened to at your convenience. You need to subscribe to receive a podcast, rather like you might subscribe to a magazine, and it is delivered at regular intervals. Podcast technology also allows you to publish audio content onto the web yourself. This is simple and affordable although you will need an internet connection, some recording software or a digital recording device, and you may need some training. One of the main benefits of podcasts is that you can listen to them in otherwise 'dead' time on your mobile phone, PDA or iPod. In addition, recording your own podcast can really contribute to your studies and transferable skills such as presentation and communication.

If you are not already familiar with the underlying technology then podcasting can seem inaccessible. To use it you need a portable audio device which you connect to a computer. You then log on to a podcasting subscription service and then subscribe to the site's feeds. You will need to have sufficient bandwidth to download the podcast.

How you actually subscribe will depend on the podcast software you have chosen. You may have heard of podcast software such as iTunes (www.apple.com/itunes), Juice Receiver (www.juicereceiver.com) or Doppler (www.dopplerradio.net) which are currently free. Alternatively, you could subscribe using a web-based feed reader such as My Yahoo or Google Reader. Again, these are free, but you will need an e-mail address to create an account.

If you have not experienced downloading a podcast before, try Activity 6.

ACTIVITY 6 Download a podcast

Log on to www.google.co.uk and set up a Google Reader account.

Now log on to www.bbc.co.uk/radio/podcasts/directory/ and choose a podcast you would like to subscribe to, following the instructions.

Either listen to the podcast on your computer or on a portable player such as an iPod, mobile phone or MP3 player, from the connection made through the USB port on your computer.

Blogs

The work 'blog' is a contraction of the word 'weblog'. Blogs are different from other websites in that they are often the comments of an individual on a topic of their particular interest. They are updated frequently, encourage readers to contribute their views by leaving comments, and can be subscribed to. Other blogs function as more personal online diaries; these are less useful in the context of academic work. In the past blogs have been mainly text based but increasingly bloggers are using pictures, video clips and sound. The collective community of all blogs is known as the 'blogosphere', and several search engines are available such as Bloglines (**www.bloglines.com**), BlogScope (**www.blogscope.net**) and Technorati (**www.technorati.com**).

In terms of academic collaboration and communication, a blog can be a great tool in reaching a project group, a team, or an audience that is spread across different locations. This is particularly useful for groups of work-based learners. It can also serve to enable collaborative work and engagement during those times between face-to-face tutorials and lectures. Blogs can also be very helpful for knowledge management. Rather than trawling through inboxes for e-mails that were sent months ago (or long ago deleted) the use of a blog's search feature can return past documents or opinions from your online community. If a discussion of a topic or project is your only aim, however, you may not need to look any further than using the discussion forums software that is available on your VLE.

Blogs are increasingly becoming a source of genuine academic discussion, peer review and knowledge sharing which could be invaluable in your study, if treated with care. Experts blogging on almost any subject can be found, either via a search engine that searches blogs like Google, or by a search of specialist engines such as Technorati. This is prompting new and useful discussions between academics across the world, who might never otherwise have become aware of each other's work.

ACTIVITY 7 Use a search engine

Log on to **technorati.com** and use their search facility to look up a subject you are currently studying.

If you would like to try blogging for yourself you will need to download specialist software, known as a blogging platform. There are a wide range of these; some are free while others are available by subscription. The easiest way to start is with a hosted blogging platform such as Blogger (**www.blogger.com**) or MSN Spaces (**http://spaces.live.com**). These have the advantage of being simple and free, but if you want a greater degree of control, or to use your own domain name, other options exist such as WordPress (**http://wordpress.org**) or Movable Type (**www.movabletype.org**).

Wikis

Your VLE is also likely to enable you to use a wiki, a website that can be built collaboratively by a group. With a wiki you can share and collaborate on documents without any special software and with the minimum of training. A wiki can be considered as work-in-progress; one person might post a rough document online and then all the others in the group can read, correct and contribute to it in real time. You can use this to support group assignments or to collaborate with others in sharing resources. The most commonly used wiki is Wikipedia (**www.wikipedia.org**), an online editable encyclopaedia, although as we have noted above, this should be used with caution.

Discussion boards

Online discussion groups can be a valuable source of information and advice, and you will be able to explore ideas and common interests. Discussions are either synchronous or asynchronous. Synchronous discussions take place in real time where a number of students log on at the same time, much like the group work mentioned in the previous chapter. These discussions will usually be organised by a convenor, such as your tutor, who may start off the discussion by posing questions. Asynchronous groups allow people to participate as and when they wish. Look beyond your own VLE's discussion groups to ready-made asynchronous groups hosted by JISC (the Joint Information Systems Committee), an independent advisory body on the use of ICT in education.

ACTIVITY 8 Access a discussion board

Log on to JISC (**www.jiscmail.ac.uk**), browse through the help/using jiscmail section, and then use the keyword search to find lists that interest you. If you decide to join a group tell other members what you are doing and why you have joined.

It is useful to check your VLE's discussion board, and e-mail system, regularly. If you use other e-mail systems then make sure your VLE e-mail is also directed to these so you do not miss any important communications.

Netiquette – a guide to good communications using technology

The principles for communication using technology are similar to those used for normal conversation, but the limitations of technology mean you need to pay specific care and attention to ensure shared understanding.

- In a computer conference you are unable to see others respond by smiling or nodding, so it is useful to acknowledge their responses by thanking them or welcoming them into the conference and asking them to contribute further. This helps to minimise isolation, but do be aware of politeness spiralling into an endless round of 'thank you'.
- It is fine to agree with points your fellow students have made, but always try to move the discussion on, rather than just saying that you agree. Try to avoid being a spectator during e-discussions by being proactive and contributing positively where you can.
- If your opinion differs, then acknowledge where your views are the same before putting your personal perspective. This will help avoid or diffuse escalating tensions.
- Ask open-ended questions relevant to your work and make sure you follow up the replies.

These final points are relevant to all aspects of writing electronic messages, whether it be in wikis, discussion boards or just e-mails at work:

- Make sure you are clear about the purpose of your message and use a precise and meaningful title in the subject line.
- Keep messages short; if you need to say something complex add a short covering message to an attachment.
- Adopt a friendly and positive tone. Remember, e-mails can be stored and may come back to haunt you. Pause before you send an angry message.
- Break the text into short paragraphs and leave blank lines, cramped messages are difficult to read.
- Before you send a message, check you are sending it to an appropriate audience. Nothing clogs up mailboxes more than the 'reply to all' option.
- Beware of using ALL CAPITAL LETTERS or lots of exclamation marks – this can give the impression you are shouting.
- Try to avoid using abbreviations or acronyms unless you are sure everyone will understand them.
- Avoid the use of emoticons (smileys), sideways-on faces constructed from keyboard characters such as :-(or ;-). Many people will not know what they signify or may not appreciate their use.

Developing your information technology skills

Debbie recommends you 'attend any extra courses offered to learn about computer skills – they can be used throughout the rest of your life.' Here are some ideas for you to try in addition to signing up for relevant workshops at work and at college:

- If you need a basic course visit **www.bbc.co.uk/webwise/learn** – this is the site for Webwise, the BBC's free basic guide to using the internet.

- www.open.ac.uk/safari/ – this is a free online course from the Open University to develop Skills in Accessing, Finding and Reviewing Information (SAFARI).
- Look at the subject benchmarking statements from the Quality Assurance Agency (QAA). These indicate the skills and knowledge expected in any graduate in a particular discipline. These can be found at www.qaa.ac.uk/academic infrastructure/benchmark/default.asp.
- Audit your skills against the key skills framework at the appropriate level for you and your work. Remember that although you may be studying for a degree level qualification (level 4), your key skills may not need to be at this level. For more information look at the Quality and Curriculum Authority's (QCA) website at www.qca.org.uk/keyskills/. Ask whether your college offers key skills accreditation.
- Make sure you incorporate the results of your audit into your CV.
- Visit the Open University's OpenLearn open content initiative for free online courses at http://openlearn.open.ac.uk.
- Consider updating your skills by enrolling on the European Computer Driving Licence (ECDL) at level 2 or the Advanced ECDL at level 3. These are known as ICDL (International) outside Europe and are useful qualifications to demonstrate your computer literacy.
- Find out what your university offers in terms of training on specialist software such as SPSS (originally Statistical Package for the Social Sciences), a package for the statistical analysis of data, or EndNote, a program for managing bibliographies. Both of these are quite advanced but may prove useful later in your studies.

References and further reading

www.ask.com/ – major search engine

www.bbc.co.uk/radio/podcasts/directory/

www.bbc.co.uk/webwise – for free online learning course

www.bl.uk – The British Library

www.blogger.com – a hosted blogging platform

www.bloglines.com Bloglines – search engine

www.blogscope.net BlogScope – search engine

http://bubl.ac.uk – Bulletin Board for Libraries (BUBL), a multi-subject gateway

http://clusty.com – meta-search engine

http://del.icio.us – a social bookmarking site

www.dogpile.com – meta-search engine

www.google.com – the largest search engine

www.intute.ac.uk – a multi-subject gateway

www.jiscmail.ac.uk – Joint Information Systems Committee, independent advisory body on the use of ICT in education

www.kartoo.com – meta-search engine

www.movabletype.org – Movable Type, a blogging platform

www.open.ac.uk/safari/ – free online course from the Open University to develop
Skills in Accessing, Finding and Reviewing Information (SAFARI)

www.open.gov.uk – UK government reports

www.qaa.ac.uk/academic infrastructure/benchmark/default.asp

http://scholar.google.co.uk/ – Google Scholar, a multi-subject gateway

www.search.yahoo.com

http://spaces.live.com – MSN Spaces, a hosted blogging platform

www.statistics.gov.uk – National Statistics Online

www.technorati.com – Technorati

http://wordpress.org – WordPress, a blogging platform

5 Preparing for research

It is almost certain that you will be expected to carry out a small-scale investigation as part of your degree course. Collecting data is one of the oldest and certainly most widely used ways in which we find out about things we want to know. Other terms to describe the process, such as 'research', 'investigation', 'enquiry' and 'study' are all used in this chapter. This may seem confusing at first, particularly as research is often associated with academics or large organisations using rigorous or complicated methods. However, it can be argued that whenever we seek to find answers to questions we are doing research. Bell (2005:2), referring to Howard and Sharp (1983), claims that research is 'seeking through methodological processes, to add to one's body of knowledge, and hopefully, that of others'.

For you as a degree student it is an initiation into an academic process which you will find of increasing value. You will, of course, have a supervisor or tutor. It makes sense for you to work closely with them. They have experience in this complex field and are able to alert you to possible ideas, problems and solutions which may save hours of confusion and unnecessary work.

As a beginner qualitative research methods, which aim to find out what people say and think and are mostly concerned with words and behaviours, may be most appropriate. However, it is useful for you to become familiar with some quantitative methods which use numerical data. Therefore the most commonly used range of methods and statistical analysis is included in the next chapter. This will be particularly important for you if, for instance, you want to understand the decisions which were made about a large piece of research you are involved in but did not design.

This chapter covers:

- preliminary issues
- gaining access to workplace data
- the research process
- determining what to research
- ethical considerations
- reviewing the literature
- ensuring validity and reliability
- choosing your research sample.

Preliminary issues

In chapters 3 and 4 you looked at ways of finding and storing information for your studies; some of these techniques will be invaluable for what follows. Your university course should have provided you with some basic training in research and you are likely to be allocated a research supervisor. There is also a wide range of texts written to guide researchers; some for those like you just starting out, others written for those engaged in post-doctoral studies. A few useful ones have been included at the end of this chapter. However, all the reading in the world will not make you skilled at data collection. In fact, there is a danger that too much information will make you indecisive and you will never get started. This chapter will alert you to the fact that everything you do must be thought through very carefully; the methodology should be rigorous and your findings should be credible and trustworthy. The following pages will help guide your thinking so that you do not end up wasting your time or, worse still, wasting your respondent's time on badly planned research. The research process is often described as being linear, in that one stage leads to another, but experience has shown that frequently it is not. One stage often overlaps with another, so although this chapter has to be written in a linear fashion you do not have to use it that way. You may prefer to dip in and out to find what you need.

Many enquiries or projects take place on someone else's territory. A poorly designed research project or enquiry could, for example, damage relationships for you in the workplace or, worse still, put people off any future involvement and make it difficult for you or other researchers. This does not mean that you have to have everything planned and organised before you start. It does mean that your research intentions will benefit from being shared with those who might be asked to give extra time, or effort, or be affected by the findings. Their collaboration may help generate enthusiasm and encourage participation, and they may give you some helpful advice.

To be an effective researcher it is important to maintain as open a mind as possible. In that way you will become aware of unexpected ideas or those which do not conform to existing accounts or theories. This involves being aware of your own values, ideas and prejudgements and is an important activity to help you avoid bias. We should ask ourselves:

'Could the research have been carried out differently?'
'Would this have given me different answers?'
'Has the way I designed the research influenced or limited what I could find?'

For Robson (2002:10) 'a principled enquiry can be of help in gaining an understanding of the human situation and its manifestations in an office, factory, school, hospital or any other environment, and in initiating sensible change and development . . . and if you can consult an expert for advice and support you may find the results are more effective.' Essentially, research findings offer a way of enhancing your existing knowledge, understanding or skill, or uncovering something new.

Gaining access to workplace data

Higher education is increasingly populated by students who are also employed. Holding down a job at the same time as studying raises a number of issues, as you have already discovered. A major advantage can be that when you come to conduct a research enquiry, you have access to arenas of potential research. For those with no connections, access is not easy and relies on countless numbers of phone calls even to be granted a conversation about the intended research. You, however, are already an 'insider'. Although this does not guarantee you access, you are more likely to know who to approach and have your request listened to. No matter how well acquainted you are with the source, you need to obtain permission to gain access to the people and resources. Staff are going to be doing you a favour. Not only do they need to know what it is you are going to do and why, but they also need to be given some idea about what they will gain by allowing you to gather data. Additionally, be realistic about what you hope to achieve. You might give false hopes, particularly if you are working with people who do not understand the constraints of research.

Academic institutions and the workplace are becoming more familiar with the potential of practitioner research and may be less likely to grant the student total freedom in deciding what to research solely on the basis of their own interests. Therefore you may find that you are expected to make a study which is relevant to the needs of your setting. This reduction in your freedom to decide is likely to be counterbalanced by a greater likelihood of being given permission to carry out research and access to resources and time.

Useful tips to help you gain access

- Request permission formally from the most appropriate senior person. A letter briefly outlining your plans and explaining that the research is part of your degree is often the best approach. Some institutions will ask for your request to be authenticated by your tutor or even a senior member of your academic institution.
- Speak to the people that you want to work with. They also need to know what you are doing and how it will involve them. If possible work as a team, sharing your observations and findings will help you to be more objective.
- Give an outline plan of the research to the person who gave the initial permission, identifying who will be involved and what they will be doing.
- Be familiar with the ethical considerations and intellectual property rights. Talk to your tutor if you are concerned.
- Seek and use the support of your research supervisor.
- If you are acting as a practitioner researcher and are conducting research which has been identified by your workplace, or will be of direct benefit to them, try to negotiate a time allowance to carry out the enquiry.

- Negotiate and agree what you mean by confidentiality and anonymity. Remember it may be possible to identify someone, even if you do not use their name.
- Agree who is going to see a copy of the final report and to what extent you are expected to share your findings.
- Be honest with the participants. For example, if you say an interview will only take ten minutes, it should.
- Dress and behave appropriately for the setting.

The research process

Research can seem a complicated process; however, it is very much like writing an essay. It has a beginning, middle and an end.

Beginning – planning

- determining what to research;
- formulating and clarifying the research question or topic.

Middle – implementation

- reviewing the literature;
- choosing the research method;
- negotiating access to the data;
- planning and conducting the research.

End – conclusion

- analysing the data;
- identifying findings and drawing conclusions;
- writing the project report or thesis.

Determining what to research

Before you can start you need some idea of what you are going to focus on. In some cases this is straightforward, particularly if you are given a topic; in which case the decision is already made for you. In others making the choice can be very difficult and this is frequently where students waste the most time. Deciding on a topic means identifying what you would like to find information about and this should, ideally, be something you are interested in. Sometimes an idea comes from work you are engaged in, an area of study which raises questions, exploring a topic you are unfamiliar with to expand your knowledge base, or a topic which is of current media or everyday interest. You may already have some data as a result of your work. This might be very helpful, but be careful that it does not act as a constraint. It could force you into deciding on a research project which later is neither of interest to you nor your employer.

> ### *Examples of ideas proposed for research*
>
> - the quality of life for newly admitted clients in a nursing home;
> - difficulties experienced by young parents who have recently moved;
> - the impact of a new road layout on the emergency services;
> - the value of assertiveness training for victims of assault;
> - implementing inclusion in secondary school;
> - why students may fail the first year of an engineering degree.

You may have a clear idea already of something you wish to find out or, more often, there may be several things which seem to be of equal importance. You can only choose one, so making a decision is the first thing you have to do.

To help you make a decision you could:

- Check a range of databases (there are some ideas at the end of the chapter) for bibliographic information about your area of interest.
- Check the titles of dissertations to see if your topic or one like it is there as they may give you clues as to what is still to be found out.
- Ask your tutor for some advice.
- Talk to colleagues at work and fellow students.

You may be asked to research as part of a group. It makes sense for each group member to have some initial thoughts first, and then to come together to discuss them and to decide on the focus. In that way everyone can feel involved in the decision-making process. It is also essential that tasks are divided and agreed, so that everyone knows what they are responsible for. This helps to build in the idea that individual thinking, group collaboration, negotiation and personal responsibility are accepted as fundamental from the beginning. If your topic has been decided for you, then clearly meetings to clarify, update and negotiate the practicalities of the topic are also essential to its success.

ACTIVITY 1 Decide on a topic

Think of a research topic and using the methods above find similar titles. Make a note of the way you found the most useful information.

Checking if you can manage the research

Is your proposal realistic and achievable?

As novice researchers we often have exciting ideas which frequently are completely unrealistic. This is often because we have not thought through the amount of information our investigation might generate. On the other hand, we may not have considered the difficulties in obtaining the data. Perhaps it is confidential and not in the public domain; perhaps it has not been recorded; or it has been recorded in a way that you will not be able to understand easily. You may not have access to the people you need to talk to. There is a whole range of obstacles which could prevent you from achieving your goal. It is essential that you look at your ideas realistically, and seek help from your tutor or colleagues in looking for solutions or alternatives.

Your degree specification and your tutor will be quite clear about your deadlines. Only you can know how quickly you are able to work. One of the most fundamental tasks you should undertake is to make a timeline. Build in extra time to accommodate those unforeseen obstacles, such as 'flu, crisis in the family and so on. Put it somewhere visible so that it acts as a permanent reminder. Be ready to make adjustments if you cannot achieve your goals. You may need to negotiate this with your tutor, so do not leave it to the last minute.

Does the topic fit within the expectations of the subject you are studying?

Although you may be given some freedom in deciding your topic, it makes no sense to research something which is not going to contribute to your knowledge of the subject. Indeed, it is often very difficult to get colleagues or research subjects to cooperate if they cannot see the relevance of a piece of research. On the other hand, you will be surprised at how helpful others can be if they consider that the results of your labours will be useful to them.

Are you interested in the topic?

This is probably the most important question to ask yourself. All research entails a certain amount of drudgery and hard work, and you will need a real interest in the subject to help you through the difficult times. However, no matter how interested you are, you do have to keep an open mind about the subject and be careful not to prejudge the answers. Discuss your proposed area of research with your supervisor and agree what the emphasis of your study will be.

Are you ready for change?

No matter how well you have planned your research and how enthusiastic you are, it pays to be ready for the unplanned. You are unwell and will not be able to observe the Early Years play group; your interview candidates are refused time to speak to you because there is a crisis on the shop floor; the supermarket is closed due to flooding; the school secretary logged an incorrect date and you were expected the previous week. The list is endless and real. Have some flexibility built in and, where possible, be prepared to substitute one activity for another. You may also have to consider downsizing the extent of the research in order to cope with reduced funding or time available.

Formulating and clarifying the research

When you have decided on your topic, planned your time and negotiated access to the data, you need to be clearer about what it is you want to find out. Usually, the easiest way to direct your thinking is to formulate questions that will help to provide you with answers. This is termed inductive research, for example

How do young people in secondary education conceptualise exclusion?

or propose a hypothesis, which is termed deductive, where an answer to a question is proposed:

The increasing rate of exclusion from secondary schools is symptomatic of the additional problems faced by young people.

Think carefully about what you want to investigate and decide on the aims of your study. For example, as a craftsperson you wish to find out if there are families where someone makes things in their spare time. Before you can start your investigation you would need to define some of your terms:

- What do you mean by 'family'? Will any group living together count?
- What do you mean by 'make'? Does repairing or putting kits together count?
- How will you define 'spare time'?
- Do you mean as a hobby? What about unemployed people?
- Will you take account of age, gender or ethnicity?
- How can you select your families?

You need to be clear because you cannot change your mind half-way through the process.

ACTIVITY 2 Think around the topic

Think of the things you need to know about the following topic before you can start to plan the research:

Does the distance travelled to an institution have an effect on student performance?

Should we rephrase this question as: 'Is there any relationship between the distance travelled by a student to their place of study and their academic achievement?' So what else did you decide? We need some definitions:

- How are we defining 'student'; will it complicate things if we accept the full age range?
- Should we have different sections for different age groups, gender and ethnicity?
- What do we mean by 'distance'?
- How are we going to define 'academic achievement'? Do we mean they get low marks? Or fail to complete work on time?
- Can we get access to this kind of data?
- How else could we get information, which might help to answer the question? We could try asking the students a series of questions. Will that help?
- We could make a survey of distances travelled by students and cross-match it with exam results. Will that give us the answer to our new question?

Finding answers to the following questions before talking to your tutor again will be helpful:

- What is your topic area?
- What do you want to find out?
- Which kinds of questions will provide you with the most accurate data?
- How will you collect the data?
- How will it be analysed?
- Who is the audience for the findings and who else may be interested?
- What contribution will your research make to knowledge?
- What are the benefits for the participants?

Ethical considerations

The next and most important stage of your research is to consider the ethical implications of your proposal. Ethics and morals are often confused, but for this book ethics are the guidelines for what we should do to conform to the codes or principles of the institutions in which we work and study. Morals are usually concerned with whether something we want to do fits within our society's notion of right and wrong. For example, we may question if it is morally right to use animals instead of humans to test baby food. On the other hand, it would be unethical to test it on the babies.

ACTIVITY 3 Consider ethics and morals

Look at the examples of initial ideas for research in the section 'Determining what to research'; consider the ethical and moral implications of each. Write them down; discuss them with friends and colleagues. Do you all agree?

Some guiding principles

Your academic institution will have ethical guidelines which you must follow. But it is worth noting the key principles:

- Consent has to be obtained from all who participate in your research; you are not allowed to involve them without their knowing. (If you are involving minors, that is people below the age of 16, permission has to be obtained from their principal carer).
- Consent usually has to be obtained from the most relevant senior person.
- Nobody should be forced or bribed to take part in research.
- Participants must be made aware of the purpose of your research, and their role in it should be made clear.
- Nobody should be asked to do something that makes them look foolish.
- Your research should not seek to change your participants, that is they must remain in control of the situation.
- Nobody should be exposed to physical or mental stress.
- Research should never invade someone's privacy.
- Participants should always be treated fairly, equally, with consideration and respect.
- Everything possible should be done to ensure anonymity and confidentiality. Again there are very strict guidelines when working with vulnerable groups such as small children, disabled people and the elderly. This is an issue that should be discussed when seeking permission.
- There should be secure methods for processing and storing any data, which should not be kept longer than necessary.

Ethical considerations are complex, you will not be expected as a novice researcher to be working alone or to have all the answers. It is assumed that your tutor will guide you, but that does not excuse you from acting responsibly and thinking very carefully about the implications of your proposed study.

Reviewing the literature

Once your initial idea has been approved you move into the implementation process. The first stage of this is to find out what already exists about aspects of your research and is called reviewing the literature. The searching and storage techniques in chapter 3 will be very useful here.

According to Robson (2002), decisions about topics for social science research are usually made after extensive reviews of the literature to find similar research, the aim being to guarantee that the new research will build on and not duplicate other work. Finding out as much as you can about your topic is invaluable. It may give you ideas about methods of gathering data you had not thought about, and it shows you what others have found out or are saying about your topic. Additionally, it makes no sense to invest a lot of time and effort into doing a piece of research, only to find out that it has already been done before and your time has been wasted. Your

Learning Resources Centre will have a range of literature, access to journals through your Athens password and can obtain texts for you. You can also use your keywords or their synonyms to locate potential sources on the internet. Here are some suggestions:

Useful databases to investigate your proposed research

- ASSIA Applied Social Sciences Index and Abstracts
- ERIC Educational Resources Information Center (international)
- BIDS Bath Information and Data Services
- BEI British Education Index (UK equivalent of ERIC)
- CINAHL Cumulative Index of Nursing and Allied Health Literature
- DisAbs Dissertation Abstracts
- Medline source for life sciences and biomedical information
- PsychINFO source for psychology and related disciplines
- Sociofile database containing sociological abstracts

This is not the case, however, for research based on the workplace. Here literature about relevant research is only investigated to provide a background. Robson (2002) sees this as change in the relationship between the researcher and the practitioner, because the researcher does not set the agenda for the research but negotiates it with the employer. Therefore a good understanding about what is already known is no longer central to the discussions. Indeed in some workplace enquiries there may be very limited or inaccessible background information or literature. There will be times when no matter how thorough your searching, there appears to be nothing written on the topic. Think creatively. There may be nothing written directly on the subject, in fact it is often highly likely, but parts of what you are looking at may exist. Use your keywords to find things that might be related to your topic. Remember to make notes about the usefulness of what you have found which will make sense to you at a later date. Always keep thorough bibliographic references and identify quotations, which you may be able to use when writing up your work.

ACTIVITY 4 Think laterally

You are planning to design some activities for a nursery class on a visit to a local art gallery. You cannot find any research on this topic. What could you look for?

You could look for research about:

- the way young children learn;
- activities for children in their early years;

- museum and gallery education;
- art education for young children in their early years;
- the value of visits for children in their early years.

So, how do you decide when you have done enough reading and searching? It is impossible to read everything, and if you tried to you would never get around to the research itself. You need to keep an eye on your schedule, so take a summary of what you have found and discuss this with your tutor, who will be able to offer you guidance on what is acceptable.

Ensuring validity and reliability

As a new researcher it is important for you to identify data gathering techniques which are manageable, easy to produce and carry out, and will give you information which is trustworthy. For your sake, and that of your workplace colleagues, you want to be confident that what you find out is worth taking notice of, and you have not been wasting your time and theirs. You need to be certain that you have tried to make sure your work is both valid and reliable. So what is meant by those terms?

To be valid the method being used should measure or describe what it is supposed to.

ACTIVITY 5 Consider research methods

Decide if the following are valid research methods:

- using a carefully recorded observation of how many people used a certain chemist shop on a Saturday afternoon to identify how many people used it each week;
- interviewing a teacher about a new method of teaching reading to tell you if it is successful;
- asking members of a Christian group their opinion of extending Sunday opening hours for their local supermarket.

You are quite correct; they are not valid research methods. Each will give either inaccurate or biased data. However, this is only a simple interpretation of the term. There is a range of other factors which can be a threat to ensuring validity. More about this issue can be found in Robson (2002:105 and 171).

Reliability is described as the extent to which the method used produces the same or similar results under identical conditions. For example, questions which ask for opinions can give results which vary from one day to the next. Unreliability can be as a result of observer or participant error or bias. There are strategies to avoid participant error, but participant bias is not easy to detect. Identifying your biases before starting research is one way to overcome this potential problem. You could also ask a colleague or your supervisor to check for consistency.

Broadly speaking your research will be one of the following:

Exploratory: You want to find out what is happening and you want to understand more. Qualitative methods are usually best for this type of enquiry.

Descriptive: You want to give an accurate picture of an event, of people or of a situation. You will need a lot of information about the topic that you are going to describe, and either qualitative or quantitative methods could be chosen.

Explanatory: You want to find an explanation for a situation or a problem and again you could use either qualitative or quantitative methods.

Choosing your research sample

Sampling is an important part of research: in any enquiry we are making judgements about people, places and things on a small proportion of what is being investigated. With all investigations the number of subjects we use will depend on the time and resources we have. However, if our data is to be useful we need to think carefully about how we select our sample. Because we depend on goodwill, we may not have total freedom to ensure our sample is perfect, and we will have to rely on what can be called random or opportunity sampling. That is, we use those who are willing and available to us. However, it is important that we mention this in the final report and try to consider how much this may have influenced the data we obtained.

So how should we make a selection? Representative sampling is when the group represents the larger population according to the criteria that will help you find the information you want. If gender and age are important to your investigation of engineering students in your college, you would ensure that you have the correct proportion to the whole in your sample. If you wanted to check the ability of children to read an instruction, you would ensure you had equal numbers of boys and girls representing the full span of reading ability within a specific age group. Whether they were tall or short would not be significant, but it would be if you were considering the correct height for school chairs.

There are times when you most definitely do not want a representative or random sample. For example, you may wish to interview the only male school teacher for infants to gain very specific insights. So, be aware that there are many other ways in which a sample can be selected. You might like to investigate this further in Robson (2002).

ACTIVITY 6 Your topic

Think carefully about your research topic. Talk to colleagues at your workplace about your research aims and ask what characteristics are essential to your sample.

Now you are ready for the following chapter which will help you to gather, refine, understand, analyse and bring your research to a useful conclusion.

References and further reading

Bell, J. (2005) *Doing Your Research Project: a guide for first-time researchers in education and social science* (4th Edition), Buckingham: Oxford University Press.

Birley, G. and Moreland, N. (1998) *A Practical Guide to Academic Research*, London: Kogan Page.

Elliott, J. (2002) 'What is applied research in education?' in *Building Research Capacity*, Issue 3.

www.jisclegal.ac.uk – for a full explanation of intellectual property rights

Robson, C. (2002) *Real World Research* (2nd Edition), Oxford, UK: Blackwell Publishing.

Trochim, W. (2005) *Ethics in Research*, London: Sage.

6 Data collection, analysis and presentation

Once you have decided on your topic, read what already exists on the subject, and considered and solved any problems of access and ethics considerations, you are ready to begin the next stage of your research. You will need to think seriously about ways in which you can collect the evidence, how to organise and understand what you have amassed, and how to analyse and present your findings so that you can draw sound conclusions.

This chapter covers:

- choosing an appropriate methodology
- qualitative data collection methods
- quantitative data collection methods
- analysing qualitative data
- analysing quantitative data
- presenting the findings
- Drawing conclusions from the data.

Choosing an appropriate methodology

Before you can decide which methods will generate the most useful data, you need to be absolutely certain about what you are trying to achieve, what you need to know and why. The following considerations are interrelated:

- Are you planning to describe, explain or understand something?
- Do you intend to find solutions to a problem you have identified?
- Are you hoping to change something as a result of your research?
- Have you defined research questions?
- How much time or funding is available?
- From whom or where are you intending to obtain data?
- What is the theoretical framework which is guiding your study?
- Are there any constraints?

The difference between qualitative and quantitative data collection methodology

There are two broad categories of data collection, quantitative and qualitative. For many years the former was the preferred way of carrying out research. Quantitative research is numerical. Researchers collect facts and study the relationship between one data set and another. It is a method which is often used to test out theories such as the effectiveness of new drugs on patients in health care, and to gather large amounts of information. Because statistical methods are used to analyse the data, quantitative research is regarded as scientific and providing reliable information. This encourages funding bodies to give considerable financial support. Additionally, quantitative data collection can be a relatively inexpensive way of undertaking market research and gauging public opinion through surveys and questionnaires. Its main weakness is that it uses very rigid methods to measure and analyse the information, so it is considered by many to be unsuited to measuring human reactions, emotions and attitudes.

Qualitative research is almost the opposite of quantitative research. Researchers using this type of data collection are more concerned with trying to gain an insight into human perception of the world. As such they recognise that it is not wise to generalise about human reactions, opinions, attitudes and so on. Additionally, in this method, the hypothesis or theory comes after the data collection. Its advantage is that it allows the researcher to make distinctions between responses, and it reports on everything that is said about a topic.

There are claims from supporters of the scientific approach that the qualitative method is weak because it often uses only quite small amounts of data and therefore its findings cannot be generalised. However, there is a growing understanding amongst the research communities that the findings from qualitative research are as reliable as those from quantitative methods. The primary disadvantage of qualitative research is that it can be quite expensive to carry out. Over the last few years there has been a growing belief that the two methods complement one another and now researchers frequently use both in the same research.

The following description of different techniques for gathering data should help you to decide which will be most appropriate for your research. They have been divided broadly into those which will give qualitative data and those which are more suitable for quantitative analysis. Some are appropriate for both. We will consider qualitative methods first as these are the ones you will most likely be using to gather your data.

Qualitative data collection methods

Case study

'Case study' is an umbrella term for a whole family of research methods:

- interviews
- observation records
- checklists of skills, behaviours, abilities, movement, procedures, inter-actions, resources
- portfolios of a range of work around a particular topic, a represent-ation of a total experience, a collection of documents for analysis
- individual files, for example tapes, samples of work, artwork, memos, photos of models or projects and reports
- diaries or journals written by participants
- field notes or informal notes
- logs of meetings, lessons, excursions, and materials used
- discussion or interaction – records of comments and thoughts gener-ated by participants
- questionnaires of attitudes, opinions, preferences, information
- audiotapes of meetings, discussions about data gathered, games, group work, interviews, groups, monologues, readings, lectures and demonstrations
- videotapes of participants engaged in their activities
- still photography of groups working, locations, faces, particular partic-ipants over time, at fixed intervals
- Time-on-task analysis of participants; over a lesson, a day, a week.

Two or three data gathering methods, or using different variables such as time of day, different teachers of the same class, are used together to provide an in-depth view of a situation. In this way findings are cross-checked and this is called triangulation. Case studies are a good method for individual researchers as they give an opportunity for a thorough study over a limited period of time. Although findings from this type of research cannot be gener-alised, that is, it cannot be seen as true for all similar situations, case studies are often used successfully to probe issues identified by large surveys.

Interviews

Interviews fall broadly into three categories:

1. In **structured** interviews there is a schedule of questions like a question-naire, to which the interviewer records the answers. This is a good technique for new researchers as it ensures they ask the same thing each time. It is also helpful for interviewing people who might find it diffi-cult to read a questionnaire.

2. A **semi-structured** interview has a schedule of questions, but the inter-viewee has an opportunity to respond to each in their own way.

Analysing the data from this type of interview is more difficult, but clearly the data may be more exciting.

3. In **unstructured** interviews only the topic is chosen. This is an excellent technique in skilled hands as the data can be really valuable, but it takes expertise to control and is very difficult to analyse.

When you are designing your interview schedule it is worth considering as a general rule that you should start with the simple questions to put your respondent at their ease. Then progress to the more difficult ones and finish with ones where respondents' opinions are important, because by then they should be more relaxed. Run a pilot interview before doing the proper research. This will give you an idea of whether the questions work, and ensure the interview does not become too long. Decide how you will record the interview; recording by hand is fine if you are working with respondents who will not be speaking at length or too quickly, but it can be distracting. Electronic recording is excellent for complex interviews and good-quality machines are essential, but it is time-consuming and costly to transcribe. Video recording is an alternative but has similar advantages and disadvantages.

Your job as an interviewer is to get people to talk freely and openly. To do this you should listen more than you speak, put questions in a clear, straightforward and non-threatening manner, avoid giving clues about your viewpoint and enjoy the experience. Try to vary your voice and facial expression and try not to look bored, even if you are. It takes skill to be good at interviewing, and this requires practice. During your preparation for this part of your degree, you should have some interviewer assessment and training, where your tutor or colleagues can provide valuable feedback. Additionally, a recording or video can enable self-evaluation.

Single person interviews

Advantages

- detailed information and opinions can be gathered;
- can be conducted in a mutually convenient and non-threatening setting;
- questions can be rephrased or explained if not understood;
- the interviewer can note ways in which the response is made such as tone of voice and facial expression;
- this is a good method when respondents cannot read or write adequately for the level of questioning.

Disadvantages

- respondent may try to please the interviewer;
- some interview settings can be very distracting;
- ethical issues of one-to-one interviews must be addressed;

- the interviewer may show a bias towards a certain viewpoint through their body language;
- wording of questions is critical;
- time-consuming.

Group Interviews

Advantages

- group interviews enable more data to be collected at once;
- group members may stimulate others' views;
- group members may feel less threatened than in a one-to-one situation.

Disadvantages

- some members of the group interviews might influence the others;
- needs careful control because discussions, though interesting, can go off the point;
- recording, transcribing and analysing interviews can be difficult.

Telephone interviews

The advantages and disadvantages of telephone interviews are the same as they are for telephone surveys which are described later on. Additionally, recording has to be effective.

Observation

Observations can be a very valuable method for data gathering. They can be structured or unstructured, concentrate on action, interaction or dialogue, or a combination of these. They can be recorded as written notes, or at intervals of time on a previously designed grid or electronically. For new researchers a structured observation schedule is very helpful. However, it does run the danger of the researcher imposing their own ideas about what they should be looking for rather than letting the events speak for themselves.

When making observations you will need to decide what role you will take:

- You can be a complete observer, sitting or standing where you have no involvement at all with what you are observing.
- If you are familiar with the situation, you might be a participant observer, watching at times and at others interacting. For example, you might be watching a physiotherapist working with a group of older patients. If you know nothing of the techniques involved you would

watch. If, however, you are experienced and the instructor is happy for you to join in, you might help some of the participants.

■ If you want to observe as a complete participant you would most likely become a member of the group you are studying. This is favoured in ethnographic research but there are ethical issues which need to be investigated.

The following theories have been included because they are part of the family of methodologies which produce data which is best analysed qualitatively. It is unlikely that a novice researcher would employ them on their own. However, if you are working collaboratively and one of these methodologies has been selected, a basic understanding could be useful.

Grounded theory

The central aim of grounded theory is to generate theory from data which is collected during the research. This is particularly useful in areas of study where there are few or no theories or concepts to describe what is going on. Data collection, analysis and theory are interspersed throughout the study. It can be applied to a range of phenomena and most commonly uses interviews to collect data. However, observation (participant or otherwise) and analysis of documents have been used. Although grounded theory is most often associated with the qualitative approach there is no reason why quantitative data collection cannot be used.

The researcher is expected to make several visits to the field to collect data, returning after each to analyse it. Visits continue until the data is saturated, that is, no new data is being added. This going back and forth from data collection to analysis is different from the traditional linear model of research where all the data is gathered and then analysed. However, it makes sense if you are trying to understand something which is complex. For further in depth understanding of this methodology see Glaser and Strauss (1967).

Ethnographic study

Anthropologists who wished to study a society or aspects of a society in depth developed the ethnographic style of research. It typically tries to answer questions about the life of specific groups or parts of groups. It seeks to capture, interpret, and explain how groups, organisations or communities live, experience and make sense of their lives and their world. This usually requires the researcher to become partially or totally immersed in the group that is being studied, and to use scrupulous participant observation. To be successful, the researcher has to become accepted as part of the group, maybe doing the same job or living in the same location over a period of time. As a method this has been criticised, partly because of the time it takes but also because it is difficult to say that what the researcher finds is typical of other groups. For example, are mechanics in a particular business typical of all mechanics?

Phenomenological research

This research focuses on the subjective experience of the individuals being studied. What is their experience? This might be, for example, the experiences of a student with disabilities in a university setting. This methodology is widely used in the field of psychology, but it is inadvisable for a novice researcher to use this approach because it uses a highly specialised vocabulary and calls for a considerable understanding.

Hermeneutics

For Robson (2002:196) hermeneutics is the 'art and science of interpretation'. It was originally used by theologians to interpret the Bible so that it could make sense to a society which was very different from the one it was originally written for. It has also been used to reinterpret texts such as the Constitution of the United States of America, to translate ideas from an eighteenth-century context to the present situation. It is now more widely used to make sense of conversations and interactions between people in different settings. Understandings are clarified by interpretation and reinterpretation. It is a system which is prone to bias, therefore detailed description of methodology is essential.

Quantitative data collection methods

Surveys

Surveys aim to obtain information that can be analysed, notice trends, make comparisons and find facts. The national census is a survey where the aim is to obtain a 100 per cent response. Most surveys are not so ambitious but this can cause problems because the sample population has to be representative. If, for instance, you wanted to find out how students who are employed manage their workload, you could not ask all students, but you could take a percentage of each age group, gender, and subject studied from various parts of the country.

In surveys, all respondents are asked the same questions and, so far as possible, in the same circumstances. Again, this is not as easy as it seems: questionnaires have to be piloted or tested first to make sure they are clear and unambiguous. Surveys can provide answers to the questions, 'What?', 'Where?', When?' and 'How?' but not 'Why?'

The advantages of surveys are that they can be a relatively cheap and easy way of obtaining large amounts of data. Sometimes, in the case of postal surveys, they are the only way of obtaining information and, of course, because they are anonymous they may encourage more honest answers. The disadvantage is that the response rate on postal and self-administered surveys is very low. Also, because they are completed anonymously, there is no guarantee that the sample represents the population. Other surveys may be influenced by the characteristics and attitudes of the interviewer.

Telephone surveys are becoming increasingly used. They have a high response rate and it is possible to ensure understanding even though there are not the visual clues as in a face-to-face interview. Their primary advantages are that distance is no problem, they are quite low in cost and they offer personal safety for both interviewer and interviewee. However, unless you already have a background in statistics, analysis is very difficult for a novice researcher.

Questionnaires

Advantages

- questions require very careful wording;
- not too time-consuming;
- anonymity of respondent is assured;
- data collector remains detached;
- can reach a large number of people;
- easy to analyse.

Disadvantages

- no opportunities for clarification of questions;
- cost of reproduction;
- cannot probe interesting responses;
- respondent must be able to read and write proficiently;
- poor response rate;
- respondent may not be telling the truth.

There are many ways in which a questionnaire can be designed, which will depend on what you want to find out. Responses can be:

- **Nominal**: Identifying your answer from a predetermined list.
- **Ordinal or Likert**: respondent selects appropriate response from a scale, for example: Law degree students should study statistics. Strongly agree/Agree/Not certain/Disagree/Strongly disagree.
- **Interval scales**: what is your age? Below 20/21–25/26–35/36–45/46–55/over 55. Circle one.

- **Ranked responses**: for example, rate the following museums and galleries visited in order of preference. Grade from 1 to 4 where 1 is the best.

  Tate Modern

  National Gallery

  Victoria and Albert Museum

  Tate Britain.

- **Semantic differential**: for example, place a tick on the line to show your opinion of the college accommodation.

  Clean_____ Dirty

Think about interviews you have taken part in or questionnaires you have completed. Consider how frustrated you have felt when you were not able to squeeze your answer into the box, or the questions were not the ones you would have asked. It is really important that you think about the way you design the questionnaire. The most common faults are:

- leading the question, asking it in a way that tells the respondent the answer;
- double questions, these give two or more choices, which may conflict;
- some questions use words which are not very precise;
- some questions are so complex they are impossible to answer properly;
- hearsay questions, these ask things about which the respondent is unlikely to have evidence, only opinion;
- closed questions which only lead to the answer 'yes' or 'no'.

ACTIVITY 1 Traps and pitfalls

Consider the following questions from a questionnaire. Which common traps and pitfalls can you identify? Can you think of another way of phrasing them?

- How much time do you spend on travelling? A great deal/quite a lot/not much.
- Which type of school does your child go to? Infant/Primary/Secondary/Comprehensive/Grammar/Other.
- Do you think your colleagues like to learn?
- Do you like to travel by train or bus?
- Should examinations at the end of compulsory schooling be easier or more difficult?
- Do you agree that men are more suited to a career in engineering?
- What do you think of the new government policy on early years education?

Experiments

The key feature of this method is that the researcher deliberately introduces some form of intervention or innovation. An example might be the introduction of an incentive system for office workers, with the view to changing their behaviour. It is reasonably easy to plan an experiment to test something measurable and, of course, most of us are familiar with the concept of laboratory experiments, where there are carefully designed procedures. It is also possible to conduct experimental research out of the laboratory, particularly in situations where there is a planned intervention or innovation. Experimental research can also be conducted by exposing one group to a planned intervention and comparing it with a parallel or control group where there has been no intervention, and noting the differences. In this instance there would have to be ethical considerations as one group could be seen as being treated better than the other. Experimental research has to be planned very carefully, but does allow for conclusions to be drawn about cause and effect. To be regarded as useful research, large groups are needed and, as such, this methodology can be expensive. For further information see Robson (2002:109–142).

Online research

It is unlikely that you would be expected to undertake online research on your own at this stage of your educational career. However, it is worth considering some of the issues surrounding this method of data collection, as clearly it is a widely used commercial tool. Online research usually takes the form of questionnaires to an e-mail address or interviews that are conducted via e-mail or through internet chat rooms. Both methods have advantages and disadvantages, which are the same as non-electronic methods. The following are those that are specific to this method only:

Advantages

- sent directly, ensuring delivery to recipient;
- easy for respondent to reply, therefore much quicker response;
- few technical skills are required;
- its novelty encourages larger response.

Disadvantages

- question design is often simplistic to ensure meaning;
- limited opportunity for interesting graphics;
- valid e-mail addresses are needed therefore anonymity cannot be assured;
- respondent has to enter data into the database and limited levels of competence may lead to entry error.

According to Eysenbach and Till (2001), definitive ethical guidelines for conducting online interviews and questionnaires have not yet been produced for the UK. Therefore, you should discuss and agree procedures for the following issues with your tutor:

- Could your research be seen as intrusive?
- Is it possible to create a closed group which requires registration to join to ensure a level of privacy and anonymity?
- Is the research community you want to contact vulnerable? For example, the mailing list of victims of violent crime or persons on drug rehabilitation programmes could be used for other purposes if it fell into the wrong hands.
- Have intellectual property rights been observed? After all, some respondents might seek publicity.
- Has informed consent been obtained?
- Will the research be valid? The potential for people to be involved in a study may be limited by lack of access to and knowledge of the internet. This is of particular significance for those wanting to use these methods for international research or with disadvantaged groups.

Action research

Action research is essentially practical problem-solving. It is carried out by a practitioner who has identified a problem in the place of work and seeks to review, evaluate and improve practice. It is carried out over a period of time and may use questionnaires, diaries, observations and so on to collect evidence. This is used to judge the effectiveness of the changes which have been implemented and to make further modifications.

The following are examples:

Will using laptops improve creative writing in my class?

As training coordinator how can I improve attendance at optional sessions?

What can I do to improve my teaching of differential calculus?

How can the motivation of assembly line workers be improved?

Other less usual methods

Documentary or content analysis

This is where a text is analysed, using either or both quantitative and qualitative methods. It can be a very useful approach, particularly if you are looking at a political, historical or educational issue. Broadly speaking, documents can be classified as one of the following:

- **Primary data:** which comes from the source at the time of the event. It may be a newspaper article or a report, a live or recorded interview, film or video footage.
- **Secondary data:** usually what was written about an event some time afterwards and includes commentaries, compilations and written texts.
- **Statistical data:** which comes from sources such as a census or survey conducted by someone else.

You do need to check:

- that you know where the document originated;
- whether the document is biased (you could still use it but need to be aware);
- that the document is representative of others created at the same time (you do have to be particularly careful about this if you are using historical documents);
- that you understand the document.

For a more detailed description of this methodology there are guidelines in Patton (1990), Robson (1998) and Cohen *et al.* (2000), which provide a range of pertinent procedures.

Diaries

Keeping a diary as part of data collection forms a common part of ethnographic or action research or case studies. It enables the researcher to supplement and triangulate other data. The danger is that diaries can become descriptive. Therefore researchers are encouraged to use their diaries to identify and reflect on 'critical incidences' and decision making. Further information can be found in Bell (2005:174–181).

ACTIVITY 2 Collection methods and problems

Look again at the examples of initial ideas for research. What data collection methods could be used? Do you see any problems with:

- The quality of life for newly admitted clients in a nursing home?
- Difficulties experienced by young parents who have recently moved?
- The impact of a new road layout on the emergency services?
- The value of assertiveness training for victims of assault?
- Implementing inclusion in the secondary school?
- Why students may fail the first year of an engineering degree?

Analysing qualitative data

Analysing the data is the central part of research; fortunately there is a wide range of approaches and techniques available to do this. Deciding which to use is not easy but sensible decisions pay dividends in the end. As a beginner, it makes sense therefore to keep in close contact with your research tutor, and to take note of their suggestions. Whatever type of data you have managed to obtain, your main task is to use it to find answers to your research. If your answers are to be trustworthy, you will have to be as unbiased as possible and have used the evidence fairly. In this way your conclusions should be able to stand up to scrutiny and alternative possibilities. Like everything else in your degree, research can all seem very daunting at the beginning, but it is exciting and you will improve with practice.

In qualitative research it is difficult to separate data collection from data analysis because there is movement backwards and forwards between obtaining the data and analysing it. Researchers often obtain data and write analytical notes about it at the time. This makes the work stronger and more reliable. Therefore it would be wise to begin to analyse your data once you start to obtain it, rather than waiting until it is all gathered in. The comparative ease of generating data is another reason for starting as soon as possible as you will certainly have more than can be dealt with at one time.

One of the main difficulties in qualitative research is the analysis itself. Although there are some researchers who see the fact that there are no hard and fast procedures as the beauty of the method, this is not helpful for you. Therefore this part of the chapter will give some basic guidelines for analysis.

Robson (2002: 374) offers some cautionary categories to bear in mind:

- **Data overload:** too much to process, remember or describe;
- **First impressions:** early input makes a big impression which leads to a refusal to change, even though later evidence does not agree;
- **Information availability:** information which is difficult to get hold of receives less attention than that which is easy to obtain;
- **Internal consistency:** tendency to ignore that which is unusual;
- **Uneven reliability:** the fact that some sources are more reliable than others is ignored;
- **Over-confidence:** the tendency to be over-confident about your judgements.

In order to analyse your data you first need to understand the language which the research participants use. Not only the formal language and jargon, but also the colloquialisms used in everyday talk. If you are taking notes, write them up immediately after the interview. If you are using a tape recorder transcribe them into a word processed document as soon as possible and print it. Either way you should have a hard copy of the exact words, grammatical errors and colloquial phrases, even non-verbal reactions if they are relevant; these give authenticity. Each should be identified with name of interviewee, date, time, location or any other data which you may later need to aid interpretation. The advantage of having hard copies is that you can read and re-read them to identify meaning, patterns and models, making analytical notes and memos. Make copies and store the masters to protect the integrity of the original documents, to allow the various components of the current analysis to be identified, and to locate the source of the comments made.

For qualitative researchers the research process is both more creative and more interactive than for those using quantitatve techniques. As you notice recurring ideas or responses you can sort them into themes. The way you identify the themes which emerge represents a movement from the descriptive, which is summarising what the interview respondent says, to the interpretative, making some attempt to identify what it all means. These processes are typical of what is sometimes called a thematic analysis.

If you are interpreting interview data the themes can be highlighted on your text in different colours or given different identifying codes. You could count the occurrences if you wanted some idea of their comparative importance. You should then group the data so that the pieces on one theme are all together. You could cut and paste them on your document; physically cut the typed transcripts in pieces and put them in folders, or create a card-index of where the references to themes can be found. Whichever method you choose you need to be sure each piece is clearly labelled so that you know who said it.

Life is rarely neatly packaged up into tidy bundles. There are always times when people go off at a tangent or odd themes arise which are not continued or are inconsistent with one another. The temptation in qualitative research is to ignore the categories that do not fit neatly into the emerging theory. All qualitative research projects will have oddments that defy characterisation. Rather than removing them from the text they need to be acknowledged as part of the whole.

ACTIVITY 3 Identify themes

Read the two responses below and identify the different things they say about the benefits of craftmaking in the curriculum. Make a list. Can these elements be grouped into smaller data sets or units of meaning?

> **Case Study** 'As far as lessons are concerned, they go absolutely smoothly, we'll lose track of time because everyone is having so much fun. Other subjects where you're doing written work, they don't get the buzz out of it they actually do with hands-on stuff. They've got their hands on and are actually capable of doing things and they're proud of it because it's actual and they are proud of what they can show. I think it gives them responsibility and they are solving problems.'

> **Case Study**
>
> Well, believe it or not, I think they get higher-order thinking skills that they don't get from other areas. Obviously the tasks do vary to a massive extent but they do a lot of their own thinking and it's higher order. I think it's important because I think we have gone past the stage where you can actually hold on to the knowledge you acquire. You have to develop your own ideas and thinking and be adaptable. There is no clear right answer, which can be a problem. The fact that you have to think practically, to solve problems, to create, to use different materials, to adapt to a situation. It does enrich them, it makes them better students; it has add-on things with other subjects.'

Now look at what we identified. Do you agree? Are there any you missed?

- hands-on;
- uses different intelligence;
- tangible outcome;
- independent learning;
- sense of pride and achievement;
- enjoyment.

We categorised these as intrinsic benefits (for the individual).

- makes learning easy;
- develops higher-order thinking skills;
- interactive and collaborative learning;
- transfer of learning;
- vocational outcome.

We categorised these as extrinsic benefits (benefits to society).

Using computer software for analysis

More recently a number of computer software packages have been developed to mechanise this 'coding' process, as well as to search and retrieve data. While some remain true to the principles of qualitative data analysis others reduce the data so that it can be analysed numerically.

- CAQDAS (Computer-Assisted Qualitative Data Analysis), which has no commercial links to any software developer or supplier, provides practical support, training and information in the use of a range of software programs.
- Microsoft NUD*IST (Non-Numerical Unstructured Data: Indexing).
- NVivo and N4 for Mac have been designed to assist qualitative data analysis. Each allows you to import and code textual data and edit the text without affecting the coding. You can also retrieve, review and

recode the data; search for combinations of words in the text or patterns in your coding; and import data from and export data to quantitative analysis software.

■ Atlas-ti is a powerful software package for the visual qualitative analysis of large bodies of textual, graphical and audio or video data.

Each software package makes assumptions about how data should be handled and care needs to be taken to be sure that the one you choose is compatible with your data. Your academic institution's Learning Resources Centre will be able to advise you of training opportunities, and may well provide you with the most up-to-date version of the software. However, as a new researcher, with a small-scale study, it may be best to use a manual approach. This will give you an insight into the intuitive aspects of analysis which are the essential basis of any methodology.

Content analysis

In content analysis you look for particular words, phrases or topics which have relevance to your research, and count how many times they appear. The data can then be recorded in numerical form and presented graphically. As such it resembles quantitative analysis and is not often used by researchers who value the richness of qualitative data.

ACTIVITY 4 Practise content analysis

Look at the transcription of an interview with a tutor who was asked to comment on working with undergraduate dissertation students. Which words occur frequently?

Case Study	'Many students in their dissertations undertake some form of qualitative research data collection exercise. This may be in the form of interviews or data collection for a larger purpose. It may be the data for a dissertation. However, most departments and programmes provide less instruction and training on how to analyse qualitative data than they do for quantitative data. Students using qualitative data analysis may be confused as to how to approach their qualitative analysis. There may not be time or opportunity for their supervisor to teach them how to use qualitative data analysis software. Alternatively, qualitative data analysis software may not be available. Given these circumstances a straightforward method of qualitative analysis is required.'

Although you have found that the most frequently occurring words are 'qualitative', 'data', 'analysis' and 'students' this would not give the full picture because references to time and concerns have not been considered.

For this reason qualitative research looks into what is being said to find other clues as to what participants really mean.

Discourse analysis

In this method data is grouped into general themes. You may have already identified some of the themes from your initial ideas about the topic. For example, pupils were asked what they thought about abstract painting before and after an intervention, where they had a series of lessons in an art gallery. Initial responses were turned into categories by the teacher. At the end of the project the pupils were asked to rate the categories. She used this data to identify the impact of her teaching.

ACTIVITY 5 Identify themes

Look at the table below. What conclusions could you draw?

	Before		After	
	Yes	No	Yes	No
I do not understand anything	12	12	5	19
I move on to the next work	17	7	9	15
I am annoyed	9	15	4	20
I am not interested in it	10	14	5	19
I want to laugh	12	12	21	3
I try to understand it	7	17	21	3
I like it	12	12	22	2

Overall you can see that the intervention has had some level of success, in that the pupils appear more willing to try to understand the paintings, were less inclined to laugh or become annoyed and appeared to like the work. However, we would not want to generalise from just this data. It would make sense for this to be triangulated with another qualitative data collection method, such as interviews or observations while on task. Another reason for cross-questioning our interpretation is that the pupils may have been particularly willing to try because they knew that they were part of a research project. This phenomenon is known as the 'Hawthorne effect'.

If you have used an action research model, presenting the data in ways described above is not really appropriate. Elliott (2002) recommends using a case study approach where all the actions are recorded and reflected on. The final report will be narrative and would normally start by outlining the purpose of the research, giving contextual details. Then it would describe and explain the methodology. The central body of the work would be an account of what went on, where the actions are reflected on. It would identify and discuss the ideas and theory that was emerging, and note the way that some of these were tested as part of the process. Finally conclusions are drawn which outline the key themes and relate them to the literature.

Analysing quantitative data

Quantitative data analysis falls into two broad categories, descriptive and inferential. With descriptive statistics you will not be concerned about other data you did not gather. It includes measures of central tendency or average and measures the variability in relation to the average. Inferential analysis, on the other hand, uses statistical tests to conjecture what might also be happening over a wider population.

The following are scores which represent the ages of the employees in your workplace:

28, 29, 37, 45, 46, 51, 54, 55, 56, 58, 58, 60, 60, 61, 63, 65

- We could say that the range is from 28 to 65 and is 37 years, and the average or mean (taken by adding all the ages together and dividing by the number of entries) is 51.6.
- As there are two mid-way numbers we find the median by adding them together and dividing by 2, giving us 55.5.
- The mode or most frequently occurring number is not often used with small sets of data. It is more difficult to define in this case as 58 and 60 occur twice.
- You could place the ages along a number line, leaving the correct spaces.
  28, 29, _, 37, _, 45, 46, _, 51, _, 55, 56, _, 58, 58, _, 60, 60, 61, _, 63, _, 65

Now you can see the variability against the average age. In this case the outlying ages in the range might be affecting the way in which we interpret this data. An interquartile range where the first and last quarters of the data are ignored may give a better picture. If you are comparing two sets of data, for example the ages of those in administrative positions with those working on the shop floor, you could take the interquartile range of both and look at the variance from the mean.

It is most unlikely that you would be expected as a new researcher to be familiar with working with all data analysis processes on your own unless you already have a qualification in using statistics. However, descriptions of them together with exercises can be found in a range of texts and websites, some of which are cited at the end of this chapter.

ACTIVITY 6 Analyse the workplace data

What can you note about the distribution of the ages of people in your workplace (see above)?

Is that significant for your research?

If you had only identified the mean age would this have made a difference to the way you interpreted this data?

The distribution along the line and the chart show that there are more people at the older age. You might infer that many will be leaving in the next few years, whereas there are relatively fewer younger employees who will have knowledge of the workplace to replace them. Why is this, do you think? Will you need other data to see if this really is a problem? If however, you had just taken the mean age of 51.6 you might have assumed that the distribution was even and there were sufficient younger employees to maintain the workforce.

As a rule quantitative data is coded by letters or numbers. For example, you want to code responses to your enquiry as to why students had enrolled for a particular module. You might code the responses like this:

It seemed interesting	Yes	No
I needed it for my career	Yes	No
It seemed easier than some of the others	Yes	No
It was the only one on offer at a time that was convenient	Yes	No
The others were full	Yes	No
None of the above	Yes	No

You might code the responses like this

	Interest	Career	Easy	Only one	Others full	None
Respondent 1	Y	N	N	Y	N	N
Respondent 2	N	N	Y	Y	Y	N
Respondent 3	N	N	N	N	N	Y

And so on. Or you could use numeric coding. The possible responses are given a code and respondents asked to circle the appropriate number, giving 1 for Yes and 0 for No:

	Interest	Career	Easy	Only one	Others full	None
	20	21	22	23	24	25
Respondent 1	1	0	0	1	0	0
Respondent 2	0	0	1	1	1	0
Respondent 3	0	0	0	0	0	1

If you wished to analyse nominal data such as asking the qualifications of your respondents, you could code as follows. A PhD could be coded 1, MPhil 2, MA 3 and so on, or it can be analysed using a tally sheet:

1 (PhD)	2 (MPhil)	3 (MA)	4 (BSc)	5 (BA)	6 (Other)
11	111	1111	1	1111	111
2	3	4	1	5	3

These results can then be transferred to a spreadsheet, analysed with the computer software mentioned above or SPSS (Statistical Package for the Social Sciences), or by hand. Again, your Learning Resources Centre should be able to provide training in their use and may offer software.

Presenting the findings

In this part of your research you are presenting what you have found out through the analysis of your data. This will most likely be presented as a table, chart or a graph using the quantitative data you have gathered, or will summarise what you have coded or organised into themes from your qualitative data. Whatever you are presenting you are not only describing what you have found but you are also reflecting on it. Typically the results section of qualitative research is larger than that of quantitative research.

Qualitative findings are presented under subheadings derived from the topics, themes or categories you developed from the analysis, many of which emerged from your review of literature. It is not a good idea to present your data question by question or to organise it so you consider each interviewee, period of observation or activity in turn. Not only does it make it very difficult to compare and contrast information but it also makes it very cumbersome and lengthy.

As you write about your ideas and make each point it is a good idea to show where your findings come from. This means including some direct quotations, excerpts or phrases which clarify your understanding of the research participants as appropriate. It will make your work richer and more interesting to read, but more importantly it helps the interpretation to be open to criticism, because it shows the reader how you interpreted it. Whenever you include quotations make sure you attribute them by giving them a code which can be looked up in the appendix so that relevant details about the speaker, situation, document and so on can be found. It is here you need to be particularly careful about not giving any clues which could lead to easy identification of the respondent, as this may run counter to your offer of anonymity. For example, teacher interviews are identified in a text as A1, A2 and so on, and additional details in the appendix give authenticity:

Code	Subject	Gender	Age	Where	When
A1	ART	F	20–29	SE	21/9/2007
A2	ART	F	30–39	NE	23/1/2008
A3	D&T	M	30–39	W	26/9/2008
A4	D&T	M	30–39	L	4/1/2007

Be wary about using too many quotations or overusing one respondent because it might appear that you are being selective and your interpretation could be seen as invalid. As you write you should also note whether your assumptions confirm or contradict what you found in the literature. You should put a few transcripts of interviews, observations, field notes and so on in your appendix as this will also help to authenticate your work.

Additionally, because there are no 'right' answers to qualitative data, it is very important for you to show how your interpretation is the most logical and plausible. This can be done by showing how you have triangulated your data or had it cross-checked for validity. Cross-checking can be done either by returning your transcripts to the participant and asking them to check it is what they said, or you could cross-check your interpretation with other researchers or your supervisor. You could find someone who is familiar with the territory yet sufficiently detached to be objective, and ask them to read your findings and conclusions. Presenting your work at a conference or student session is also another way to ascertain if your interpretations are plausible.

There will be times when it is possible to convert your data to a visual representation. This will enable understanding of how assumptions of the data were arrived at. For example, the following chart identified what a known number of teachers would recommend to their chair of governors to enable them to work effectively with teaching assistants.

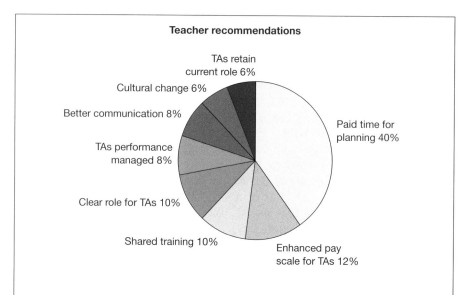

Teacher recommendations

- TAs retain current role 6%
- Cultural change 6%
- Better communication 8%
- TAs performance managed 8%
- Clear role for TAs 10%
- Shared training 10%
- Paid time for planning 40%
- Enhanced pay scale for TAs 12%

The authors wrote:

'Other resource issues included enhanced pay for teaching assistants, money for performance management and an increase in numbers of teaching assistants throughout the school . . . there were comments relating to the need for mutual respect and ensuring that teaching assistants are treated as full members of the school and have access to all facilities. However, respondents were concerned that poor definition of teaching assistant roles and teaching assistants not being resourced to cover attendance at meetings after school were likely to become problematic. Respondents wanted to see the provision of regular, planned and paid meeting time for teachers and teaching assistants, as well as specific training programmes for the latter.'

Source: Wilson, E. and Bedford, D. (2008) 'New Partnerships for Learning': teachers and teaching assistants working together in schools – the way forward', *Journal of Education for Teaching*, 34:2, 137–150. Reproduced with permission.

Quantitative findings are presented as charts, tables, diagrams and so on. Each is described, the analysis procedures explained, and the reader reminded of the hypothesis or control measures which have been put in place. Significant findings are identified and reflected on in the same way as the presentation of qualitative data.

Drawing conclusions from the data

This final part of data analysis is where the circle is completed. You started with a hypothesis or a series of questions. You read around the subject, designed a method of gathering data to enable you to find out more about your topic. You carried out your research. You analysed and discussed your data and identified emerging themes. Now, after a simple and clear restatement of your research problem or questions and your results, it is time to draw conclusions.

You should begin by discussing your findings and relating them back to the problems you identified in the introduction. This should not be a repetition of what you have already written. With qualitative research you should consider whether you can now add anything new, as a result of what you have just found. With quantitative research methods you would make a statement of what has been found. You should consider what the implications are for the wider world. You should also identify any counter-arguments or unanswered questions. You can draw interesting conclusions even from a small study, so long as you remember there is a big difference between generalising about your findings, which you cannot do, and relating ideas to a wider context.

It is also at this point that you should evaluate your research, noting ways in which you tried to ensure it was both valid and reliable. You should also consider any limitations to its design, the effects they may have had on your findings, and areas which need to be explored in the future. You might finish by discussing the implications for policy and practice for you or those who were involved: your workplace or your educational institution, for instance. Remember to exercise a little sensitivity here, particularly where questions have been raised about working practice or the need for changes in policy. There are ways in which these can be identified without damaging your relationship with your employer or institution. For example, the teachers' recommendations to enable them to work effectively with their teaching assistants were summarised in the conclusion, as follows:

Our findings reinforced Dixon's (2003) assertion that a key issue was the resourcing of non-contact time for teachers and their teaching assistants to plan together; with a significant number of questionnaire respondents and interviewees stating that their key recommendation would be paid time in school hours for planning and liaison. Several of the questionnaire respondents stated that a funded enhanced pay scale for teaching assistants was a key recommendation they would make to their headteacher or governing body. This reinforced the review of literature where a finding was that the pay differential between teachers and their teaching assistants made partnership difficult (Moyles and Suschitzky, 2003, Parker and Townsend, 2005).

Source: Wilson, E. and Bedford, D. (2008) 'New Partnerships for Learning': teachers and teaching assistants working together in schools – the way forward', *Journal of Education for Teaching*, 34:2, 137–150.

References and further reading

Bell, J. (2005) *Doing Your Research Project: a guide for first-time researchers in education and social science* (4th Edition), Buckingham: Oxford University Press.

Birley, G. and Moreland, N. (1998) *A Practical Guide to Academic Research,* London: Kogan Page.

Cohen, L., Manion, L. and Morrison, K. (2000) *Research Methods in Education* (5th Edition), London: Routledge & Falmer.

Denzin, N. and Lincoln, Y. (eds) (2000) *Handbook of Qualitative Research* (2nd Edition), London: Sage.

Elliott, J. (2002) 'What is applied research in education?' in *Building Research Capacity*, Issue 3.

Eysenbach, G. and Till, J.E. (2001) 'Ethical issues in qualitative research on internet communities', *British Medical Journal* 323 (7321), 1103–5.

Foddy, W. (1995) *Constructing Questions for Interviews and Questionnaires,* Cambridge: Cambridge University Press.

Glaser, B. and Strauss, A. (1967) *The Discovery of Grounded Theory*, Chicago: Aldine.

http://hsc.uwe.ac.uk/dataanalysis/quantWhat.asp – University of Bristol site provides helpful information about quantitative data analysis and many examples to work through.

www.inspiringlearningforall.gov.uk/measuring_learning/steps_in_the_process/analyse_data/

www.intute.ac.uk/socialsciences/ – useful papers on qualitative analysis.

Patton, M. (1990) *Qualitative Evaluation and Research Methods* (2nd Edition), London: Sage.

Robson, C. (2002) *Real World Research* (2nd Edition), UK: Blackwell Publishing.

Stephen, M. (2006) *Teach Yourself Basic Computer Skills*, London: McGraw-Hill.

Wilson, E. and Bedford, D. (2008) 'New Partnerships for Learning': teachers and teaching assistants working together in schools – the way forward', *Journal of Education for Teaching*, 34:2, 137–150.

7 Quotations, citations and bibliographies

Many of you will be writing an academic essay or report for the first time. The key difference between academic work and the writing you have done previously is that you have to demonstrate that you not only understand the topic but have drawn on a range of sources to verify, challenge, critique and add to your existing knowledge. Additionally, the whole idea of academic writing is that it builds on the work of others and can be built upon by others, thus extending knowledge. You will therefore want to demonstrate your wider reading on, and knowledge and understanding of, your topic by including material and ideas from other sources. These may include diagrams, tables, charts, written arguments, theoretical positions, research, policy documents, statistics and so on, as well as notes taken by or given to you during lectures. All must be professionally referenced and included in the bibliography.

Academic institutions vary in their regulations concerning the inclusion and acknowledgement of the work of others and will have issued you with guidelines as to their preferred system. Referencing may seem tedious but should not be left to the end of your writing. You should become familiar with the correct system for your academic discipline from the start; it is easy to invent your own method which later has to be unlearned. Further, it is easy to forget where your ideas and arguments came from. You can waste a lot of time as you play detective at the end.

All academic institutions are quite clear – failure to acknowledge sources is regarded as plagiarism and may result in your work receiving no marks and could result in disciplinary action. As this is such an important topic there is a separate section dedicated to it (see page 116).

This chapter covers:

- why you need to cite your sources
- quotation in the text
- how to cite work in the text
- using and citing electronic material
- footnotes and endnotes
- compiling a bibliography
- electronic bibliographic management
- how to avoid plagiarism.

Why you need to cite your sources

So why is an acknowledgement of sources, meticulously cross-referenced to a bibliography, so important?

- It lets your reader know where you found ideas and information.
- It allows you to return to your work at a later date and revisit some of your ideas using the texts and sources you identified.
- It allows others who read your work to find your sources and use them in their work to extend their ideas.
- It is good manners to acknowledge the work of others.

Case Study	Julie reminds us: 'Every thought and statement has been thought of or written before, so ensure you read before and then reference.' Lisa-Marie adds: 'Always show recognition of other people's ideas and views, reference your quotes and the ideas you got from reading.'

Therefore whatever system you use, it should be clear, consistent and helpful.

Quotation in the text

Using quotations is an excellent way to give authenticity to a piece of work. Used selectively it can help to bring a text alive by allowing another voice to add to or critique your ideas. If you followed our suggestions in chapter 3 you will already have identified from your reading some powerful and pertinent quotations. Clearly these must all be referenced in such a way that they can be checked. Some academic disciplines have very specific rules, so you must consult your course handbook or check with your tutor. Your academic institution will also most likely offer guidelines as to the percentage of words in your work which can be a direct quotation (between five and ten per cent is the norm).

There is a danger that using a quotation can be a substitute for saying something you are experiencing difficulty in expressing. Sadly, it is a trap inexperienced writers fall into and although it may seem an attractive option, it is not acceptable. All quotations should be preceded or followed by an interpretation in your own words that indicates to your reader how you are using it. There is a whole range of conventions and techniques to enable you to include direct quoting in your text without it seeming clumsy, whilst allowing your reader to visit your sources.

- All quotations should be exact, including grammatical errors. You can put '[sic]' immediately after the mistake to indicate that you have quoted correctly and the mistake is not yours.
- If you want to leave irrelevant words or phrases out of a quotation you should use an ellipsis '. . .' (three dots) in their place.

- You can add your own words to make the meaning clearer but these should be placed in square brackets.
- Usually quotations of up to 30 words are included in the text in quotation marks. Longer ones are indented and single spaced. Again, academic institutions vary in the style they specify.
- In all cases the author, date and page number(s) are given.
- If you are quoting from in-house journals or publications you should check if permission is required.

Incorporating quotations into your writing

Please note that many of the examples below are fictitious. Only those from original sources relevant to your learning have been quoted in the bibliography

You might want to use some single words to give strength to your work:

> Bedford (2007:19) criticised the work of outgoing students as 'sloppy' and 'poorly conceived'.

Or you may use a whole phrase, with your understanding identified at the beginning:

> In consideration of the standard of student work, Wilson (2007:213) suggested that 'the claims that student work was "sloppy . . . and poorly conceived" in Bedford (2007:19) were exaggerated and based upon limited observation'.

Or a whole phrase with an interpretation following:

> 'Obtaining reliable statistical data regarding student standards year on year is problematic' (Wilson, 2007:213). Therefore claims regarding poor standards should be viewed with caution.

The second sentence is the student's interpretation of the quotation.

For longer quotations there are no quotation marks and the details are given at the end. Again, an interpretation should precede or follow.

> There are a variety of courses available to students who are undertaking work-based learning. However, it is vital that they are sufficiently flexible to enable students to construct programmes which provide them with relevant qualifications at the same time as keeping as close to the workplace as possible (Midshire University, 2006:10).

Quoting numerical data

There are two forms of numerical data you may wish to quote in your work:

1. **Raw data** such as that drawn from a workplace. For example, numbers of employees and hours worked, which may later be used to complete government or internal statistics for analysis.

2. **Statistics** that have previously been prepared.

Both must be acknowledged in the same way as a text and are most likely to require you to seek permission if the data you wish to use is likely to be published. With workplace statistics permission should be sought and the necessary precautions taken to ensure anonymity. Remember, theft of trade secrets is not only to be found in novels; it does exist and data can be misappropriated. You cannot assume that your paper or dissertation will not be used by rival workplaces to their advantage.

Quoting statistics from other research also needs to be treated with care. It is essential you check their validity and the data is reliable. Please check chapter 5 if you need to remind yourself of these terms. If you are in any doubt about the data, words of caution should be added in your text. Obviously, sources should be accurately cited.

- Formulae should be indented and referenced in such a way that they can be cross-checked from your compiled list.
- Numbers in the text from one to ten are written in words and from 11 upwards figures are used.
- High numbers are written as words, for example, 'one thousand'.
- Figures are used for dates, times, currency and technical information, such as '20mm brush'.
- Tables, charts, diagrams and so on should be identified and allocated a number according to the order in which they appear in your text. Each should have a title and any other labelling needed to enable your reader to interpret the data. Check whether these should be listed separately.

Including visual material

Including photographs, charts, diagrams, reproductions of artworks, cartoons and images from other sources can be a powerful way of enhancing your work. The rules for referencing them are exactly the same as for quotations; after all, they were not created by you. Everything must be acknowledged. You might, for instance, want to include a structural diagram of the Parthenon for an essay you are writing about classical architecture, or as an example of early diagrammatic idioms. Whatever your purpose, your reader should be able to identify your source. Remember, with visual material the ethics of use are the same as those which apply to all other data. Permissions must be sought and royalties paid, if necessary. Anonymity must be assured if the image can be misappropriated. This is particularly relevant where photographs of children and vulnerable people might be identifiable. Failure to observe these ethics could result in severe penalties for you and your academic institution and in the workplace.

How to cite work in the text

This section investigates referencing. You will also learn how to acknowledge sources which you have used but not quoted from – this is called 'citation'. Neglecting to acknowledge the ideas of others or indicate where you obtained your information is the most common reason why students are failed for plagiarism. It may be easy to overlook the fact that many of your ideas came from someone else once you have written your essay or assignment. All ideas which are not yours must be cited.

You need to do this when you:

- quote or use exact words from another source in your writing;
- summarise or express views which are not your own;
- paraphrase material from another source;
- copy diagrams, tables, formulae and so on.

In sentences where the information is prominent, the author and date of publication are cited at the end of the relevant sentence or paragraph, in parentheses, and separated by a comma. The full stop comes after the parenthesis. Note, only the author surname is used even if the first name is known:

> The unseasonably cold weather was responsible for the significant surge in energy consumption (Bedford, 1989).

In sentences which have been constructed using the work of more than one author, each author's name is placed immediately after their particular contribution:

> The unseasonably cold weather (Wilson, 1990) was responsible for the unusual surge in energy consumption (National Statistics, 1989).

Where the ideas are based on a number of studies, all are acknowledged in ascending date order, separated by semicolons:

> Alcohol consumption has increased predominantly among young people (Adam, 2005; James, 2007; Forson, 2008).

In author-prominent sentences, the author name occurs as part of the text and only the date is in parentheses:

> According to Bedford (1989), the unseasonably cold weather . . .

Or the date can be included as part of the sentence:

> In 1989, Bedford identified from her research that the unseasonably cold weather . . .

If the author has more than one publication for a particular year, a lower case alphabetical denominator is used. This is allocated in order of publication if you know it, or in the order they are used in your text (Wilson, 1995a). Consistency is really important here, which is another very good reason for building your bibliography at the same time as your essay.

If the text has two authors, both are cited (James and Jackson, 1997); where there are more than two, 'et al.' is used (Bedford et al., 2005). However, all names are included in the bibliography.

Where no author is cited, 'anon.' with date accessed is acceptable. Again, if there is more than one anonymous work an alphabetical denominator is used.

There are times when you come across a text cited by another author that you want to use; as a general rule you should try to locate the original, using their bibliographic reference in order to check that the citation is neither misquoted nor misinterpreted. It does happen. This can present difficulties, particularly if the work is out of print, in another language or very old. Additionally, you may have a time limit imposed by the submission date of your assignment. In these cases it is important that you make clear to your reader that you are not citing from the original document. This is achieved in one of the following ways:

> Bedford (1999), citing the work of Youngman (1925), indicated that there had been many changes in provision of health care
>
> Youngman (1925), cited in Bedford (1999), researched provision of health care . . .
>
> Bedford (1999) cites Youngman (1925) in reflecting on the changes . . .

This system also applies to any reference you may make to prefaces, forewords, introductions or afterwords by one author in the work of another.

Some authors use 'ibid.' (short for ibidem, Latin for 'in the same place') or 'op. cit.' (which is short for either opus citatum 'the work quoted' or opere citato 'in the work quoted') to save giving the full details each time. This can be very frustrating for your reader as they track back to see which reference it was you used last therefore its practice is discouraged.

Using and citing electronic material

You may wish to use a wide range of electronic materials in your text, such as:

- a website, web page or e-learning material
- journal or newspaper accessed through a website or database

- e-mail
- CD Rom or DVD
- chat room.

As previously noted the internet is an excellent source of information, used wisely. At present there are no agreed standards for quoting from or citing electronic sources. Therefore it makes sense at the moment to adopt the same techniques used for quoting or citing a written text. If you are intending to submit your work to a scholarly journal you should check their preferred method of citation. Whatever you do you should be consistent, and it is imperative you always acknowledge your sources. Plagiarism from an internet source is possibly the easiest for your academic institution to detect and many universities use anti-plagiarism software such as Turnitin.

Many sites can be identified by the author and the date when the work was written and this is how it will be identified in your bibliography. However, not all sites can be identified by an author; sometimes they are papers from another academic institution, the government or a range of organisations. In these cases it is usual to put the name of the site and the date of the paper. Where there is no date the name of the originator is sufficient. If you are quoting from the paper and there are no page numbers you should use the page number identified by your computer screen. Remember, you are trying to make it as easy as possible for someone else to find your sources. More about this topic and detailed examples can be found in the section on compiling a bibliography (see page 112).

Footnotes and endnotes

Footnotes are notes where a superscript number – [1] – or a number in parenthesis – (1) – replaces an in-text citation, and the full details of the source are placed at the foot of the page as well as in a bibliography. In some cases the notes may be placed at the end of the chapter or the whole work; these are referred to as endnotes. Footnotes and endnotes should not be used together and care is needed in their use as too many can be distracting. Superscript numbers run consecutively throughout the text and remain outside your punctuation, whereas numbers in parenthesis stay inside. They are usually placed at the end of the sentence or at a logical break if there is more than one.

The advantages of using footnotes are that the text is not interrupted and more bibliographic detail and relevant comments can be included. These might otherwise interrupt the flow of your writing. Footnotes can also be used to make a cross-reference to another part of your text. However, it could be argued that additional data should only be included if it is relevant, and should form part of the text or be included in the appendix. Footnotes should not duplicate what is already clear in the text. Again, there is some debate as to whether footnotes should be used so make sure you check what your academic institution prefers before making a decision. This may vary between subject disciplines. For further information Gloucester University website has useful notes about using them.

Compiling a bibliography

Different systems for referencing and bibliographies

You should begin this task as soon as you start reading and gathering data for a piece of work. It also makes sense for you to add in any other potentially useful reference material you come across by chance. Check how your academic institution states how your sources should be presented. Some prefer you to separate out only those you referred to within your work; these are titled 'References' and should be presented separately from those which you only consulted. Other institutions like to see everything presented in the one 'Bibliography'. Until you become familiar with your texts it makes sense to write a short descriptive note if it is not clear from the title. Remember you should omit this later. For example:

> Skilbeck, M. (1985) School-based *Curriculum Development*, London: Harper and Row. Ch 5 useful critique of development of National Curriculum for schools.

Make referencing your golden rule of writing and whichever system you use make this the second part of your golden rule: all references cited in your text should be immediately placed in your bibliography.

Case Study	Margaret suggests: 'Every time I find something of interest I may use I write who and where, etc. and put it in my bibliography', and Subiratha said: 'Every time I quoted or wrote a statement of fact, I'd highlight it, number it and on a separate page I would write where I obtained the information'.

Your bibliography will contain all the books, texts, papers and other sources you have used to produce your piece of work in alphabetical order by author's surname. Your college or university may have a particular style and there are a number of variations. The most common referencing methods are:

- Harvard
- Modern Languages Association (MLA)
- Vancouver
- Chicago.

The Harvard system

The Harvard system appears to have become the standard form of referencing at most academic institutions in the United Kingdom so we will concentrate on it in this book. It enables your reader to find the material you used and is written as follows:

- author surname, comma
- author initial(s), full stop, ed./eds if it is an edited text
- year of publication in parentheses
- title of work in *italics* (or underlined if handwritten), comma
- edition if not the first
- place and/or country where published (either or both are acceptable), colon
- publisher, full stop.

For example:

Gregory, R. L. (1977) *Eye and Brain*, London: Weidenfield and Nicholson.

Grundy, S. (1987) *Curriculum: Product or Praxis?* Lewes, UK: Falmer.

Longer entries may have a hanging indent; either the second and subsequent lines are indented, or the first line is indented five character spaces from the left margin, as below. Also note how two authors are cited:

Graham, D. and Tyler, D. (1993) *A Lesson for Us All: The Making of the National Curriculum*, London: Routledge.

Although in your text you write '*et al.*' to indicate a source that has more than two authors, they are all included in the bibliographic reference. Commas are used to separate each name and placed after the initial and full stop:

Taylor, S., Rizvi, F., Lingard, B. and Henry, M. (1997) *Educational Policy and The Politics of Change*, London: Routledge.

If you have more than one text for an author they appear in date order, with the earliest first. Where they have published more than one text in a year, each year date is given an alphabetical suffix attributed either by order of publication or, if unknown, the order in which they appear in your script.

If you have cited an author who has contributed to an edited book it looks like this:

Greenhalgh, P. (1997) 'The history of craft', in Dormer, P. (ed.) *The Culture of Craft: Status and Future*, Manchester, UK: Manchester University Press.

You also need to indicate if it is a second or further edition:

Robson, C. (2002) *Real World Research*, 2nd ed, UK: Blackwell Publishing.

Sometimes you will be referring to an unpublished work or lecture presentation:

> Grace, G. (2000) 'The state and the teachers: problems in teacher supply, retention and morale'. Paper presented at Regional Dimensions in Teacher Supply and Retention Conference, University of North London, 19 January.
> Guba, E. G. (1978) 'Towards a methodology of naturalistic inquiry in educational evaluation', CSE Monograph Series in Evaluation No. 8, Los Angeles: University of California, Centre for Study of Evaluation.

If referring to a newspaper or journal article, note how the article title is indicated by quotation marks and the journal or paper is italicised in these examples:

> Hacker, R. G. and Rowe, M. J. (1998) 'A longitudinal study of the effects of implementing a National Curriculum project on classroom processes', *The Curriculum Journal*, vol. 9, no. 2, pp. 95–103.
> Hague, H. (1998) 'Fears for future as craft classes are axed', *Times Educational Supplement*, 3 April, p. 25.

Usually we do not need to include standard dictionaries and encyclopaedias in the bibliography. However, on occasion it is important for the reader to find your source of information. Where there is no obvious author cite as much detail as possible:

> *Education Authorities Directory* (1995), England: The School Government Publishing Co. Ltd.

Referencing electronic sources

An electronic reference should indicate not only the website but also the date on which you accessed it. Sometimes it is difficult to find all the information but it should include as much as possible from the following list:

- author's name and initial if known
- available from URL (the '**http://**' may be left off if the URL also contains '**www**')
- title of item, in quotation marks
- title of complete site or work (if relevant), in *italics* or underlined if handwritten
- followed by '[online]'
- date of publication or last revision date, if there is no date put '[n.d.]'
- date of access, in square brackets.

Here is an example:

> Robinson, B. (19/07/1996), 'End of the World Predictions', *The End of the World is Nigh* [online] available from www.onbridgeconsultants.com [accessed 31/12/1999].

If the reference is within an online journal, the same rules for journals and books apply.

For a personal e-mail, with attachment:

> Macadam, M., m.macadam594@concept.ac.uk Fwd. *Campus news*, sent 24/01/04 [accessed 25/01/04].

You may want to reference videos, audiotapes, CD-ROMS, television and radio programmes or computer software. The general principles are the same as for books, but if there is no author or obvious title you will have to decide what to use as the keyword and how much detail to give about the programme. An organisation could be used as the keyword.

Electronic bibliographic management

Commercial products are also available for storing details of references. There are several programmes, such as EndNote and Reference Manager. These databases enable you to store, manage and search for references in your own database. You will need to balance the effort, time and cost you invest in these systems against the benefits. References from your database can be inserted into a word-processing document and used to create your bibliography in an electronic format. You can input your own references or import information via your Athens account from online bibliographic data-bases such as BIDS, EBSCO and so on without needing to retype them.

Such packages allow you to enter information about each reference in fields you set up. You can also store abstracts, notes and keywords. You can then extract groups of references by using the fields you set up. For example, you may have categorised your entries by age of text, whether the text is based on research or not, the specific topic and if it was published in the UK or not. The programme could extract references to all research less than ten years old carried out in the UK on a topic you identify and present them in a separate bibliography which you can import into your work.

Most higher education institutions will have purchased a licence for such a programme which will be available for you to install on your computer. Your Learning Resources Centre will be able to help. For more information about these useful tools look at commercial packages such as EndNote (**www.endnote.com**) and Reference Manager (**www.refman.com**).

How to avoid plagiarism

Plagiarism is the intentional or unintentional use of another person's work as if it were your own. This not only includes written and printed work but also all visual material and information from electronic sources. Note that many institutions may penalise a student for unintentional plagiarism as harshly as if it were deliberate. The best a student can hope for in that instance is an interview with senior university personnel where they will be given an opportunity to explain their actions, before a final decision is made. As previously mentioned, it is to be avoided at all costs. Not only is it an extremely dishonest practice and can be seen as stealing, but it carries considerable risk for you. Most higher education institutions require their students to submit an electronic version as well as a paper copy of their work. They have a programme which can detect work that is similar to other students in any of the institutions that have the software. It can also detect material copy-pasted from websites, journal articles and so on. Lecturers are also skilled in spotting plagiarism through years of experience of reading and marking work. Avoiding detection should not, of course, be your primary reason for not plagiarising.

Case Study	Lynda says: 'Reference, reference, reference. Include all books, pages, papers and quotes. Never pretend you said something that you didn't. It is so obvious and you will be found out.'

For those of you who are new to the concept of academic writing, it is understandable that you may find difficulty in recognising that researching and citing the work of others is a strength, not a weakness. Using the work of others to support and challenge your own ideas is preferable to ignoring it as it increases the objectivity of your work.

Case Study	Emma says: 'Reference your quotes so you know you are not using another person's ideas as your own.'

There are very strict guidelines in most HE institutions to ensure you acknowledge all your sources. All the following are seen as plagiarism:

- quoting words with no reference;
- citing a source without acknowledging where exact words have been used;
- paraphrasing;
- using some words, intertwined with your own, with no reference;
- blending from more than one source without acknowledgment;
- citing your source but not including it in your bibliography;

- using all or part of an unpublished work, such as a student paper or lecture notes, including those you have made yourself;
- writing a piece of work with someone else and not acknowledging them;
- working together with another student and using the same words or recognisable phrases.

ACTIVITY 1 How to identify plagiarism

Consider the following extract about museum use and the three examples of ways in which students may have used this information in their writing. Can you identify which are plagiarised?

With increasing funding pressures to widen their audience, museums are beginning to see the potential in attracting very young children and their families. In the early 1990s Walsall's 'Start' programme designed and experimented with art gallery space for under-fives (Cox, 1995), and more recently a series of workshops called 'Big and Small, Short and Tall' was run by Tate Britain for under-threes and their parents (Hancock and Cox, 2002) . . . They were both characterised by interactive 'hands-on' strategies, welcoming parents and building on children's existing knowledge, using a thematic approach (MacRae, 2007:159).

Example 1

Museums can see the potential of encouraging young people and their families as a means of gaining funding and pressure to increase the numbers that attend. Start, a programme designed in the 1990s in Walsall made a programme for children under five, and, more recently, Tate Britain ran workshops for children under three with their families. Both emphasised an active approach and used the children's prior knowledge (MacRae, 2007).

Example 2

Creating programmes for young children and their families has been used by museums as a means of responding to increasing funding pressures to widen their audience. Walsall's Start programme in the 1990s and Tate Britain's Big and Small, Short and Tall are examples. These were characterised by interactive hands-on strategies and building on children's existing knowledge (MacRae, 2007:159).

Example 3

My research has discovered that many museums are creating programmes targeting and welcoming children under five and their families. This is because they see them as audiences of the future and they need to improve their funding. The thematic programmes are usually of a practical nature and use the children's knowledge and understanding.

- In the first example, the student has paraphrased the extract. Although exact words were not used, it is so close to the original in sense and construction that it should have been acknowledged by giving page numbers.
- In Example 2 the student has used many of the exact words without indicating with quotation marks which ones were used.
- Example 3 has used much of the information in the extract to create a paragraph but the source of the information has not been given. Indeed, the student has claimed it as their own.

Were you surprised? Students tend to think of plagiarism as direct copying without acknowledgement. These examples are, however, quite common in student writing.

Sources which should be acknowledged

- advertisement (film, television or radio)
- art exhibition
- article (sometimes anonymous) in a work of reference
- article from online periodical
- article in a learned journal
- article in a newspaper or magazine
- article in an edited collection
- audio recording (LP, CD, audio tape)
- audio recording (private)
- book by a single author
- book by more than one author
- book comprising an edited collection of articles
- book which is part of a series
- book with no author identified
- chapter of a book
- computer program (e.g. game)
- conference proceedings edited by one or more editors (published)
- conference proceedings edited by one or more editors (unpublished)
- document from internet site
- edition by one author of the works (e.g. essays, poems, letters) of another author
- editorial in a periodical (anonymous or otherwise)
- e-mail message
- feature film (perhaps on video or DVD)
- internet site (entire site)
- interview (already transcribed/edited into print or not)

- item or sequence of items in an anthology
- live performance (concert, play)
- map
- message from online discussion forum or news group
- multi-volume work
- museum or exhibition catalogue
- online book (whole text or extract)
- pamphlet
- paper from conference proceedings
- periodical article on CD-ROM
- published letter
- reference work on CD-ROM
- reprinted or republished book
- section of a book
- specific edition of a book
- television or radio programme
- unpublished dissertation
- unpublished letter
- untitled review in periodical (learned journal or newspaper)
- work of art (e.g. paintings, photographs).

References and further reading

www.glos.ac.uk/departments/lis/referencing/footnotes/

Greenhill, A. and Fletcher, G. (eds) (2003) *Electronic references and scholarly citations of internet sources* [online] – available from: www.spaceless.com/WWWVL/ [accessed 14/08/08].

www.leeds.ac.uk/library/training/referencing

MacRae, C. (2007) 'Using Sense To Make Sense Of Art: young children in art galleries', *Early Years*, Vol 27.2, 159–170.

8 Techniques for academic writing

Success on most higher education courses will depend, to a large extent, on the quality of the written material you submit. If you look at your course handbook you will see that you are expected to produce written work in the form of assignments. Some may be professionally orientated, such as portfolios and business reports; this mode of writing is designed to address the needs of your specific vocational situation. Other writing will be more academic, such as essays and dissertations, which aim to focus on debates about theoretical perspectives.

Although each of these types of writing has specific conventions, what they have in common is that they require you to develop a writing style that may be very different from that which you are used to. However, it is essential to know what standard is expected of you at each level of undergraduate study, and how these academic levels inform the specific marking schemes for your degree.

For your degree you will be expected to answer specific questions and to present your evidence in a logical sequence. You will need to deal with conflicting arguments and take a precise and objective stance – quite a challenge for even the most confident and experienced writer. In our experience, everyone struggles with their first written assignment, so we will take you through the process step by step. Remember, you won't be able to achieve an effortless academic writing style straight away, but hopefully our advice on the conventions of writing for academic purposes will start you off well. Your tutors' comments on your written work will help you to develop your writing over the course of your degree. Indeed, when you look back over your studies you may find that your ability to write more effectively is one of your most significant achievements.

This chapter covers:

- expectations of undergraduate level writing
- understanding generic assessment criteria and marking schemes
- managing the writing process for producing assignments
- preparing for your first essay
- writing for academic purposes – some practical guidance
- the process of writing your essay
- writing reports and dissertations.

Expectations of undergraduate-level writing

When writing at undergraduate level you will need to demonstrate that you can think clearly and critically, use valid evidence and produce well-structured and coherent written work. This applies broadly to all academic disciplines. Writing at university is likely to be different from the writing you have done at school or in the workplace. For example, at work a concise listing of key points might suffice to answer a query. As a student you will be expected to elaborate on points with argument and explanation, based on your reading and other investigations.

It is clearly the case that many students are unsure about exactly what they have to achieve at each level, so the Quality Assurance Agency (QAA) has produced two frameworks for HE qualifications, one for England, Wales and Northern Ireland and one for Scotland. These frameworks are concerned with the level of qualifications and the associated knowledge and skills students should have. A brief guide to the level of academic qualifications can be found below, and further information is available from the QAA website (**www.qaa.ac.uk/academicinfrastructure/FHEQ**).

A brief guide to academic qualifications

The higher education qualifications awarded by universities and colleges in England, Wales and Northern Ireland are at five levels. In ascending order, these are the Certificate of Higher Education (level 4), Foundation Degree (level 5), Bachelor's Degree with Honours (level 6), Master's Degree (level 7) and Doctoral Degree (level 8).

Certificate of Higher Education level 4

The holder of a Certificate of Higher Education will have a sound knowledge of the basic concepts of a subject, and will have learned how to take different approaches to solving problems. They will be able to communicate accurately, and will have the qualities needed for employment requiring the exercise of some personal responsibility.

The Certificate may be a first step towards obtaining higher level qualifications.

Foundation Degree level 5

Holders of qualifications at this level will have developed a sound understanding of the principles in their field of study, and will have learned to apply those principles more widely. Through this, they will have learned to evaluate the appropriateness of different approaches to solving problems. Their studies may well have had a vocational orientation, for example, HNDs enabling them to perform effectively in their chosen field.

They will have the qualities necessary for employment in situations requiring the exercise of personal responsibility and decision making.

▶

> ### Bachelor's Degree with Honours level 6
>
> An Honours graduate will have developed an understanding of a complex body of knowledge, some of it at the current boundaries of an academic discipline. Through this, the graduate will have developed analytical techniques and problem-solving skills that can be applied in many types of employment. The graduate will be able to evaluate evidence, arguments and assumptions, to reach sound judgements, and to communicate effectively.
>
> An Honours graduate should have the qualities needed for employment in situations requiring the exercise of personal responsibility, and decision making in complex and unpredictable circumstances.
>
> Source: QAA (2008) *The Framework for Higher Education Qualifications in England, Wales and Northern Ireland,* Quality Assurance Agency for Higher Education. Reproduced with permission.

Information on the specific skills that an honours graduate might be expected to have can be found in the QAA subject benchmark statements. These set out expectations about standards of degrees in a range of subject areas.

ACTIVITY 1 Check your level

Look at the information about subject benchmark statements on the QAA website under the section on academic infrastructure. Select the appropriate statement for your degree and read about the level of communication skills a graduate with an honours degree might be expected to have.

Understanding generic assessment criteria and marking schemes

Assessment criteria inform the assessment process by providing a link between academic standards as set at the level of the award, and academic standards at module level. Assessment criteria are written in a language that is general, reflecting the *Framework for Higher Education Qualifications* (FHEQ) (QAA, 2001). Assessment criteria are not to be confused with marking schemes. Assessment criteria identify student achievement of generic learning outcomes in the broadest possible terms. They correlate three key variables – level of learning, marking standards, and student achievement – in a taxonomy of statements about assessment. Have a look at the example from Anglia Ruskin University in Figure 8.1 to see how this works.

Generic Learning Outcomes	Assessment criteria by level	Marking standards (by mark band)					
		70%+ Distinction	60–69% Merit	50–59% Pass	40–49% Marginal Pass	30–39% Marginal Fail	1–29% Fail
Knowledge, Understanding and Intellectual Skills	**Level 1 (certificate)** introduces students to HE. Students are expected to demonstrate relevant skills and competencies; to be articulate in expressing ideas orally; and to be coherent and structured in terms of written or other media. Forms of expression at this level may be descriptive or imitative, but students are expected to demonstrate an increasing understanding of the theoretical	Excellent information base, exploring and analysing the discipline, its theory and ethical issues with considerable originality. Very good academic/intellectual skills	Good information base; explores and analyses the discipline, its theory and ethical issues with some originality. Good academic/intellectual skills	Satisfactory information base that begins to explore and analyse the discipline and its ethical issues but is still mainly imitative. Acceptable academic/intellectual skills	Basic information base; omissions in understanding of major/ethical issues. Largely imitative. Some difficulties with academic/intellectual skills	Limited information base; limited understanding of discipline and its ethical dimension. Weak academic/intellectual skills	Inadequate information base; lack of understanding of discipline and its ethical dimension. Wholly imitative. Very weak academic/intellectual skills
Transferable and Practical Skills	background of their study and the analytic competence to explore it, as well as its relationship, where appropriate, to particular skills. Students are expected to develop an awareness of strengths and weaknesses in their skill sets	Excellent management of learning resources, complemented by self-direction/exploration. Structured/accurate expression. Very good team/practical/professional skills	Good management of learning resources with some self-direction. Structured and mainly accurate expression. Good team/practical/professional skills	Satisfactory use of learning resources and input to team work. Some lack of structure/accuracy in expression. Satisfactory practical/professional skills	Basic use of learning resources with no self-direction. Some input to team work. Some difficulty with structure and accuracy in expression. Developing practical/professional skills	Limited use of learning resources, no self-direction, little input to team work and difficulty with structure/accuracy in expression. Practical/professional skills are not yet secure	Inadequate use of learning resources. Failure to contribute to team work. Major problems with structure/accuracy in expression. Very weak practical/professional skills

A mark of 0% may be awarded for non-submission, plagiarism, dangerous practice, incoherent and insufficient work, and in situations where the student fails completely to address the assignment brief and related learning outcomes

Figure E.1 Sample generic assessment criteria and marking standards at level 1

Source: Anglia Ruskin University, with permission.

A marking scheme is used at module level to inform the first marking and internal and external moderation of each item of assessment. Marking schemes identify the knowledge and skills which students must demonstrate to achieve the learning outcomes of the module. They are used to calculate the total mark to be awarded for an individual item of assessment. Generic assessment criteria inform the writing of marking schemes, ensuring that they are broadly comparable across the institution and the HE sector.

To facilitate consistency first markers will refer closely to the marking scheme when marking your work. They pass the marking scheme on to the internal moderator/second marker and eventually to the external examiner with your scripts. This should enable all parties to understand the basis on which marks are awarded, and lends a fundamental transparency to the assessment process.

A sample marking scheme is shown as Figure 8.2. This is for an intermediate level (HE2) module in Communications at Work from Oxford Brookes University where students are required to produce a portfolio. All marking schemes will vary, depending on the task set and the presentation guidelines of the institution. It is essential that you are aware of how you will be assessed for each module, so do make sure you always look at the marking scheme before starting any piece of assessed work. If at all unsure, discuss it with your module or personal tutor.

ACTIVITY 2 Analyse and compare marketing schemes

Look at the marking scheme shown in Figure 2, paying particular attention to the criteria for communication and presentation. Compare this to the marking schemes from your HE institution.

Managing the writing process for producing assignments

Although styles of writing do vary to some extent between subject areas, there are some basic techniques that apply to all. This section of the book aims to take you through the step by step process of producing your first written assignment, from starting with a title to finishing with the feedback from your tutor. Writing an assignment is not one task, it is several, and you need to plan the process so you allow adequate time for each step. As soon as you are set your first written assignment you need to start thinking about what is required so that you can focus your reading and begin to make notes about anything that might be useful.

An early start is essential; often the assessments from different modules end up with the same deadlines and you will have to learn how to juggle

Mark	Knowledge/Understanding (40%)	Application of Theory (40%)	Communication and Presentation (20%)
70+	Detailed knowledge and understanding of a wide range of key ideas/concepts relating to workplace communication. Assignment demonstrates evidence of critical and original thinking	Portfolio entries apply a range of concepts studied on the course and reveal awareness of the broader context. Evidence of attempt to apply these critically and independently in a selection of workplace documents	Writes fluently and effectively, clarity of expression is excellent. Good structure and presentation with consistently accurate grammar, spelling and punctuation. Persuasive for task and audience. Harvard referencing relevant, clear and consistently accurate.
60–69%	Good knowledge and sound understanding of a range of key ideas/concepts related to workplace communication. Insightful thinking and work	Portfolio entries apply some of the concepts covered on the course, revealing some awareness of the broader context. Concepts not always applied critically and with evidence of independent thought	Clear structure and flow, work is well presented. Grammar, spelling and punctuation essentially accurate. Appropriate for task and audience. Harvard referencing mostly correct and consistent throughout.
50–59	Some key ideas/concepts understood. Appropriate levels of thinking	Portfolio entries apply some of the concepts covered in the course, but reveal little awareness of the broader context. Little evidence of independent thought	Adequate structure and presentation. Some errors of grammar, spelling and punctuation. Relates to task and audience. Harvard referencing errors evident but of minor nature.
40–49	Some attempt to use ideas/concepts. Some evidence of understanding	Portfolio entries make very little reference to concepts covered on the course and are heavily based on previous experience of workplace writing	Weak structure and presentation, stilted writing style. Grammar and/or spelling and/or punctuation poor. Harvard referencing present but contains inaccuracies and inconsistencies
Fail	Ideas/concepts introduced during the module not used, confused or misunderstood	Portfolio entries make no attempt to refer to concepts covered on the course	Poor structure leading to incoherent work. Grammar and/or spelling and/or punctuation consistently poor. Harvard referencing has major inconsistencies/inaccuracies or is absent

Figure 8.2 Sample marking scheme

Source: Oxford Brookes University, reproduced with permission.

your tasks. The sooner you start the better. It avoids stress in the longer term, and helps you present the best possible piece of work you can accomplish at this stage of your degree.

Case Study	Pauline recommends that you 'use your time wisely, gather information and start work promptly. Don't leave it to the last minute or you will have sleepless nights.'

ACTIVITY 3 Plan your timetable

For each assessed task you should identify the due date and today's date. Then work out your deadlines using a calendar. Always allow time for the unexpected, and take into consideration other work and personal deadlines. Put dates next to the following headings:

- analysing the task
- preliminary reading
- planning the format
- first draft
- editing and final proof-reading
- final printing and presentation.

Now read through the sections below, up to and including the essential checklist before submission of any written work. After doing so you may wish to revise your plan.

Preparing for your first essay

Analyse the question

Time spent understanding the elements of the task and planning your response is never wasted. The title should set you thinking about the material you have been studying. It is essential to show by your final paragraph that you have answered the question, or completed the task, posed by the title. It is important when you first receive your title to pick out the key words. These fall into two categories:

- content-related words, which give you an idea of what you should write about, setting useful parameters;
- instruction words, which tell you what approach you should use.

> ### *Essay title example*
>
> Review the arguments for and against the use of qualitative and quantitative approaches to research in your own work setting.
>
> The key content words and phrases in this example are: 'qualitative and quantitative approaches to research' and 'your own work setting'.
>
> The key instruction words are: 'review', 'arguments for and against'.

ACTIVITY 4 Analyse your essay title

Write down the essay title you have been given and circle the key content-related words. Now look for the instruction words from the list below. Do you understand exactly what you have been asked to do by your tutor? Check any words in the title you don't understand in a dictionary, encyclopaedia or a general reference text for your subject, and write down their definitions.

> ### *Key instruction words*
>
> - **Account for**: give a good explanation of something and evaluate possible causes/reasons.
> - **Analyse**: examine the topic by dividing it into parts, look at each part in detail, form judgements about each element and the whole.
> - **Apply**: put a theory into operation.
> - **Argue**: provide reasons for and/or against something, in an appropriate order, citing evidence, which may be other people's research, or other kinds of facts and information.
> - **Assess**: judge the significance of something, referring to the special knowledge of experts wherever possible, that is referring to or quoting from other people's work.
> - **Comment on**: give your own opinion about something, supported by reasons and evidence.
> - **Compare**: examine one thing in relation to something else, to emphasise points of difference or similarity.
> - **Consider**: give you views on, supported by reasons and evidence.
> - **Contrast**: explore the differences between the items or arguments mentioned.
> - **Criticise**: discuss the weak and/or strong qualities of theories or opinions, supporting your judgement with reasons and evidence.
> - **Define**: explain the exact meaning of a word or phrase.

▶

- **Describe**: give a detailed account of different aspects, points of view, parts, characteristics or qualities.
- **Discuss**: consider something by writing about it from different points of view with supporting evidence.
- **Distinguish**: look for differences between.
- **Enumerate**: list and mention items separately in number order.
- **Evaluate**: calculate the value, validity or effectiveness of a theory or decision or object and so on, including your own opinion, and supporting each point with evidence of specific facts, details or reasons.
- **Examine**: critically explore the opinion or argument.
- **Exemplify**: show by giving examples.
- **Expand**: give more information about.
- **Explain**: give reasons how and why to account for something, so it is clear and easy to understand.
- **Identify**: pinpoint or list.
- **Illustrate**: use examples or diagrams to make explicit.
- **Indicate**: point out, but not in great detail.
- **Interpret**: give your own opinion of the significance of something, citing reasons and evidence wherever possible.
- **Justify**: give good reasons for decisions or conclusions, perhaps by referring to other texts.
- **Narrate**: indicate what has happened in the way that you would tell a story.
- **Outline**: give the main features, facts, or general idea of something, omitting minor details.
- **Plan**: show how to organise something.
- **Prove**: show something is accurate or true or valid by using facts, documents and/or other information to build your case.
- **Reconcile**: show how apparently conflicting things can appear similar or compatible.
- **Relate**: establish how things are connected or associated, how they affect each other or how they are alike.
- **Report**: give an account of a process or event.
- **Review**: examine an area and assess it critically.
- **Show**: explain something giving evidence or examples to establish a strong case.
- **Specify**: give details of something.
- **State**: put something clearly and concisely, support each point with specific facts or details.
- **Summarise**: give a brief, concise account of the main points of something leaving out details and examples.

▶

- **To what extent**: consider how far something is true or not true.
- **Trace**: follow the cause or stages in development of something in chronological order from its start.
- **Work out**: find a solution to a problem.

Gathering your ideas together

There will be time for reading what others have to say about the topic later, now is the time for some thinking. When gathering your ideas you should note down everything you think about the topic, without stopping to consider the merit of each idea. It is creative, easy and you will begin to get some ideas down on paper.

Case Study	Kerry suggests you produce 'spidergrams of areas you want to write about in your assignments'.

It is essential that you begin writing your ideas down now, even if you later discard most of this. As your list gets longer you should begin to feel more confident about writing your assignment.

Case Study	Charles advises that 'the worst part is putting pen to paper. Once you get started it's not as bad as you think it is. Always ask for help if you're struggling.'

ACTIVITY 5 Visualise your thoughts

Take your annotated title and write it in the middle of a large sheet of paper. Now jot down any thoughts at all as they come to you. A good way to do this is on large Post-it notes, as you can later move these around into some form of structure. Write quickly and uncritically. If you prefer, you can use a mind map or a spider diagram to complete this task. For further information on these techniques see chapter 3. If you are stuck for ideas try and jot down thoughts about:

- points for and against the question in the title;
- what each of the key content and instruction words mean;
- which areas you need to develop;
- what examples or illustrations you can give;
- what further reading you need to do;
- which areas need references.

Producing an essay plan

Now you have plenty of ideas, it is important to get them into some kind of shape. At this early stage in your studies this does not have to be over-complex. Each part of the essay structure will be considered in more detail later in this chapter. You would do well to be mindful of Aristotle's advice on writing classical drama: there should be a beginning, a middle and an end.

Academic writing should always present a logical sequence of ideas, and you should use information as evidence to support or contradict your point of view. You should be looking to do more than just describe; a sound essay shows that you can see more than one side to a question. This is a good way to demonstrate your ability to analyse and evaluate information. To obtain high marks it is necessary to demonstrate these skills. The trick is not to devote too much time to the descriptive element at the expense of analysis and argument. You should show that your argument is based on evidence, not on unsubstantiated opinion. The argument should flow through the title, from sentence to sentence, to the conclusion, without any breaks. Some hints on how to structure your essay into key paragraphs are given below.

The structure may look like this:

- introduction to tell the reader what you are going to do;
- first argument for: state, support, explain;
- second argument for: state, support, explain;
- first argument against: state, support, explain;
- second argument against: state, support, explain;
- make judgements on evidence;
- conclusions;
- references and bibliography (this is covered in detail in Chapter 7).

Alternatively, your 2000-word essay could look like this:

- introduction (200 words);
- state main topic one: evidence for/against, explain (400 words);
- state main topic two: evidence for/against, explain (400 words);
- state main topic three: evidence for/against, explain (400 words);
- make judgements on evidence (300 words);
- conclusions (300 words);
- references and bibliography.

At this stage you may also want to allocate a rough word count against each section, as in the example above. This is arbitrary, but it may help you keep within the word limit. The purpose of the word limit is to train you to be con-cise in your writing. Your academic institution will usually tolerate a 10 per cent variation on the word count, but may penalise you if you stray more than this. Do check the minimum and maximum word limits before you submit, your work. Also make sure you know how to use the word count facility on your word processor. If you use Microsoft Word have a look at the floating word-count toolbar from 'Tools > Word Count > Show Toolbar'. Now, have a go with your ideas from the idea-gathering exercise in Activity 5:

ACTIVITY 6 Organise your ideas

Take the Post-it notes on which you have written your ideas. Try to organise them into sets of arguments, evidence or comment. These will eventually be your paragraphs. Can you see a logical sequence gradually emerging?

Now summarise this into your essay plan.

Now do some targeted reading

You now need to go and do some reading, and the best place to start is with the notes you have made and handouts you have been given. At this stage your tutor is likely to be concerned about whether you understand the course content. However, in higher education you will be expected to read more widely than using a single core textbook so look at the suggestions for further reading, and search journals and other online sources. Do not spend too long reading; make sure you allow sufficient time for writing the essay. Prolonging your reading beyond your scheduled deadline could be a strategy to avoid writing.

ACTIVITY 7 Reading

Now is the time to read purposefully. Do not be sidetracked, search systematically for evidence to support your arguments, remembering the advice in chapter 3.

Make very brief notes of what you have found in the appropriate place in your essay plan and note down references, as shown in the previous chapter.

Revise the order of your essay plan if necessary.

Writing for academic purposes – some practical guidance

There are a number of accepted conventions which you should follow when writing for academic purposes. This will involve writing in a formal but hopefully readable and interesting style, with a minimum of jargon. A useful maxim might be: write to express and not to impress. Consider the following guidelines.

The use of personal pronouns

One of the most common questions asked by students is whether it is appropriate to write in the 'first person', that is, using the word 'I' in an assignment or essay. Academic writing should be based on reason and argument, so generally you should avoid using personal pronouns, such as 'I' and 'we', as this can appear subjective and biased. Your personal involvement with the subject should not overshadow the importance of what you are commenting on or reporting. You can avoid the perception of bias by using impersonal language. This is called using the passive voice, for example, 'it may be considered. . .', rather than the active voice, 'I consider . . .' Be aware that the grammar checkers in some word-processing packages suggest that passive expressions should be changed to active.

The situation here is complicated, however, and there is no straightforward, correct answer. In some subjects, particularly Education and the Arts, you may be expected to write about your personal experience, or to apply academic work to your own practice. Disciplines such as science are usually much less personal. Regardless of the subject you will need to write in a balanced, informed way. The best way to tackle this is to check with your tutor first as, in our experience, many tutors have strong preferences and this differs between disciplines.

Take care with emphasis

As just outlined, academic writing focuses on intellect rather than emotion, so you need to take care when you wish to emphasise a point. Do avoid subjective, personal words such as 'great', 'nice', 'unusual', which may mean something very different to your reader than they do to you. Be cautious about using absolute terms such as 'always' and 'never' unless you are certain of your ground. We would also suggest that you should not:

- use bigger type to emphasise something;
- use bold or italics to emphasise a point;
- put in exclamations like 'Cool!'; or
- use exclamation marks.

Avoid colloquialisms and slang

A colloquialism is any feature of language which is commonly used in speech but not in writing, except perhaps in e-mails and informal notes. In colloquial English there is sometimes a tendency to misuse tenses and to concentrate on the present tense. The past tense should be used in academic writing to describe or comment on what has already happened.

- **Slang words:** like the exclamation 'Awesome!' carry a lot of local meanings and associations and so are not exact enough to use in academic argument.
- **Contractions:** words like 'they're' for 'they are', or 'isn't' for 'is not', should be avoided and written out in full. Texting contractions are also inappropriate and should not be used.
- **Abbreviations:** should be avoided. They are fine for note taking but should not be used in formal academic writing. Again, write words out

in full, use 'for example' not 'e.g.', 'namely' and not 'viz.', 'that is' and not 'i.e.' and so on. You should avoid 'etc' and also the ampersand '&' for 'and'; neither belongs in formal academic writing.

■ **Split infinitives:** although common in everyday speech, should be avoided in academic writing. A commonly quoted split infinitive is from the opening sequence of *Star Trek*, where the mission of the Starship Enterprise is 'to boldly go where no man has gone before'. The infinitive, 'to go', has been split by the adverb 'boldly', so the grammatically cor-rect phrase would be 'to go boldly'.

Always write in complete sentences

A sentence is a self-contained unit of meaning, starting with a capital letter and ending with a full stop or question mark. As a minimum it has a verb, a 'doing' word, and a subject, a person or thing that is carrying out the 'doing'. By reading your work aloud you should be able to tell whether yo' sentences can stand by themselves or whether something is missing. T practical ability to judge what works is more important than a det' knowledge of the rules of grammar. Another way to check is to us' word-processing package's grammar-checking facility. In Microsc you should click on 'Tools' and then 'Spelling and Grammar'. It good Idea to vary the length of your sentences as this is prob reader-friendly than line after line of unbroken text.

Understand how to punctuate

Punctuation is essential to help the reader understand is a very brief guide to some of the punctuation issue tant and sometimes overlooked by students. We number of books to help you with punctuation, c end of this chapter. The most accessible and a *Leaves* by Lynne Truss (2003) which is well wort'

Capital letters

Capital letters should be used at the nouns, such as words that name spec' so on. Common nouns, words that 'teachers' or 'university' are not cap' where each letter stands for a wh academic convention is that the alternative it should be written ' ately after the full title, thereaf'

Apostrophes

The two main uses of apostrophes are to indicate possession, or the omission of letters or numbers. When an 's' is put at the end of the word to indicate possession or ownership, then there should always be an apostrophe before it. There is an exception if the word already ends in an 's' because it is plural. In that case you add the apostrophe to indicate possession, but not another 's', for example, 'students' union'. Note there is no apostrophe required for 'its' to indicate possession.

We have explained above that contractions such as 'wasn't' should not be used in academic writing as they are too informal. However, it is quite correct to use an apostrophe in everyday writing to indicate that you have left letters out ('it's' for 'it is', 'it has'). Similarly, 1970s can be abbreviated to '70s.

Other punctuation marks

Brackets There are three types of brackets, otherwise known as parentheses. Round brackets () are used to isolate explanatory information. They can be over-used so check if they can be replaced with commas. Square brackets [ ] should be used for adding words within a quotation. Curly brackets {} are used in maths and computing for specific purposes.

Comma (,) There are few rules for the use of a comma, as its use is often a matter of taste or emphasis. The basic function of a comma is to separate words, phrases or clauses in a sentence, when its sense demands a slight pause. You might be able to appreciate this better if you read your work aloud. If you feel a need to take a breath mid-sentence, then a comma is probably needed, or even a full stop and a new sentence. However, many writers over-use commas in a way that interrupts the flow of a sentence, so you should use a comma only when it contributes something to the sense.

Colon (:) Use a colon to introduce lists at the beginning of a sentence. The follow-on words in the list should begin with lower-case letters and each item in the list should be finished with a semi-colon (;) except the final point which finishes with a full stop. Colons should also be used to indicate a long quotation (over 30 words) which is then indented in the text. Finally, a colon can be used to lead from one clause to another: such as from a statement to an example (as here).

Ellipsis (. . .) These three dots mark words omitted from a quotation (for example, 'The boy stood on the . . . deck'). Ellipsis marks should be three dots, no more.

Exclamation marks (!) These indicate shock or strong feelings and are rarely appropriate in academic writing. They can be replaced with a full stop.

Full stop (.) A full stop should mark the end of a sentence. It also marks an abbreviation where the last letter of the abbreviation is not the last letter of the complete word, so p.a. and m.p.h. are correct but Dr. (a contraction)

Hyphen (-) Use for prefixes (for example, ex-colleague), to join numbers and fractions (for example, seventy-one, three-quarters) and to join a single letter to an existing word (for example, E-Type).

Italics (*italics*) These should be used to differentiate text to show titles of publications (*War and Peace*), species (*Homo sapiens*) and foreign words (*et al.*)

Inverted commas Use 'single quotation marks' to mark the exact words printed in a text or spoken. 'Double quotation marks' place a quotation within another quotation.

Semi-colons (;) These should be used to separate listed items when the description uses several words. They should also be used to separate two or more clauses of equal importance.

Question mark (?) This is placed at the end of an interrogative sentence. It has the force of a full stop and should be followed by a capital letter. Do not use a question mark and a full stop.

Spelling

You should always use your word processor's spellchecker before you submit any piece of course work. However, be aware that a spellchecker does not pick up properly spelled words which may be incorrect in your particular context, 'fro' instead of 'from', for example, or 'there', 'their' or 'they're'. These latter words are known as 'homophones', they sound alike but have different spellings and meanings.

ACTIVITY 8 Homophones and common confusions

Look at the list below of homophones and words that are commonly confused and make sure you can define them. If you are not sure then look up the answers in a dictionary and make a note for future use:

affect/effect	forward/foreword
cite/sight/site	practice/practise
complement/compliment	principal/principle
discreet/discrete	stationary/stationery

As you cannot rely entirely on a spellchecker it is essential to make time to read your work through, preferably aloud, before submission. Reading aloud can really help you to spot mistakes, particularly missing words and repetitions. If you have used any word you are not sure of then look it up in a dictionary.

ACTIVITY 9 Spelling

Ask someone to read you the list of commonly misspelled words below, and just check how many you can spell accurately. It is worth keeping a list of the mistakes you make most often in the back of a diary or file, and adding to it as necessary.

accommodation	advertisement	aesthetic	assessor
beginning	calendar	coefficient	commitment
comparative	definite	dilemma	grammar
government	independence	knowledge	liaison
lieutenant	omission	precede	privilege
psychology	restaurant	sentence	separate
sergeant	sincerely	supersede	unnecessary

Avoid discriminatory language

You should not use language that discriminates against people in your academic writing, and this means you need to think consciously about sexism, racism and disability. Much discriminatory language is unintentional, and here are some hints on how to write appropriately:

- Do not use words that assume all people are male: 'people' is better than 'mankind', reception can be 'staffed' rather than 'manned'. You could use the phrase 'he or she', or even 's/he', but this feels rather clumsy. This can be avoided by turning the sentence into the plural and using 'they'.
- Avoid using job titles which assume the person is male or female. Use 'supervisor' rather than 'foreman', for example, or 'police-officer' rather than 'policewoman'.
- Avoid using racist and disablist language. Again, this is often done in ignorance. Have a look at the British Sociological Association's guidelines on language. You will find these under equality and ethics resources on **www.britsoc.co.uk/equality**. They also have useful information about non-sexist language.

The process of writing your essay

Writing your opening paragraph

It seems obvious to start writing with the opening paragraph but we are going to suggest you leave the detail of this until you have finished drafting the rest of the essay. Your introductory and concluding paragraphs are the most important, so we suggest you just read through this section, start work on the main body, then come back and write the introduction last.

The most important point we would make is that under no circumstances should you merely repeat the essay title. Paraphrasing the question is empty and unnecessary. What you should do instead is to make sure you:

- say how you plan to address the topic. Look back at the instruction-related words here and list the key stages of the essay so that the reader knows what to expect and in which order;
- establish some control over the subject, perhaps you wish to focus on a specific area or contest a particular viewpoint. This is particularly important if the word limit means you will not be able to cover all aspects comprehensively;
- indicate why the topic of the essay is important or interesting, perhaps making reference to some published work or a range of arguments about the subject;
- define key words if they are unclear or ambiguous. Make sure you say something about your interpretation of the definition. If, for example, there are several different definitions, this then would be worthy of comment. Use this technique with care.

These are the basic principles and you can use them in any order. You could also consider beginning with a quotation. This can address the third point above and, if chosen well, can be an interesting and lively way to start.

Writing the main body of your essay

Here you need to follow the plan you made, writing paragraph by paragraph to ensure you bring out the key points. Remember you are looking to state, support and explain. So, always check that every point you make is supported by evidence. This evidence must be accurately referenced (see chapter 7 for further details).

Does your argument hold together? Your essay must move convincingly from point to point. When planning it can be useful to use subheadings although these should be removed in a later draft. In most essays subheadings are not used, although they are used sometimes in the social sciences or for very long essays, so check with your tutor. Each paragraph needs to be written so it is self-contained and is one topic or element in the argument. Then give each coherence by linking them together to develop the argument in a way that is clear for the reader to follow. One way to do this is to begin a new paragraph with a link back to the previous one, then connect that in some way with the new topic.

Links can function as signposts and can be of many different kinds. You might want to:

Add something: add to what you've just said, using words such as again, also, as well as, and, furthermore, in addition, moreover, next;

Make comparisons: compared with, likewise, in the same way;

Show some form of contrast: to what you have said: although, but, despite, even though, however, on the contrary, on the other hand, nevertheless, yet;

▶

> **Make a concession**: although, even though, however, whilst;
>
> **Give examples**: as an illustration, for example, for instance, in this case, namely, one example is;
>
> **Emphasise**: certainly, definitely, especially, indeed, in fact, particularly, unquestionably, without doubt, such as, thus;
>
> **Show argument**: although, as a result, at this point, because, consequently, evidently, hence, however, moreover, since, therefore, thus;
>
> **Conclude**: as a conclusion, as has been stated, finally, in general, in short, on the whole, to sum up.

Certain signpost words are most frequently used at the beginning of a sentence. These include: for example, furthermore, however, moreover, nevertheless. These should be followed with a comma.

ACTIVITY 10 The middle

Now write the main body of your essay, following your essay plan. Just do the best you can, there should be time left for redrafting later. If you get stuck with your writing have a look at the section on how to deal with writer's block.

Writing a concluding paragraph

Your first and last impressions are crucial. You need to show your reader that you have answered the question; the easiest way to do this is to return directly to the essay title, using one of the conclusion links above. You must make your viewpoint clear here, by briefly restating your argument, perhaps putting in a last quotation, then making a final judgement in your own words. If you do use a quotation, do not let it speak for you, remember you should be in control of the essay. Furthermore, you should not introduce new ideas in the conclusion that have not already been discussed in the main body of work. Other interesting endings include:

- a very short final sentence to contrast with your detailed argument earlier in the essay;
- a comment about gaps in current knowledge or putting your argument into a wider context.

ACTIVITY 11 The end

Now write your final paragraph, then go back and write your opening paragraph. Put your writing away at least overnight. Do not hand your work in, it will almost certainly need redrafting.

Coping with writer's block

If you feel anxious about your writing, it is quite possible you will suffer from writer's block, where the words just will not come. Everyone suffers from it at times, here are some tips about how to beat it:

- Distract yourself by doing something completely different. Positive suggestions include taking a relaxing bath, going outside for a walk or doing some work in the garden. In a way it does not matter what displacement activity you choose; just stop writing and do something completely different for at least half an hour.
- Reading your work aloud often helps you make amendments to what you have written. By proof-reading and amending your existing work you may get back into writing again.
- Write a paragraph, or write for 15 minutes without correcting your words, nothing more, and then allow yourself to stop and do something completely different.
- Try the technique of leaving a sentence or paragraph unfinished where you know exactly what you will write when you return. That way you can start off your next writing session fairly easily.
- Try explaining the structure of your essay to a friend or a family member. You will probably need to simplify your ideas and language and their enthusiasm might give you some ideas and motivate you to start writing again.

Writing your second draft

You now need to revise your first draft. To do so you must ask yourself the following questions:

- How does the essay match up to the assignment criteria? Read through the criteria and identify any areas of weakness and then address them.
- Does the essay have an effective introduction and conclusion? These are key areas to work on as they are the first and last things your reader will see. So go back and tighten up your writing.
- Is your argument always supported by evidence? Do not skimp on this, is there any final reading you need to do?
- Does your argument flow clearly? Highlighting the key point in each paragraph will help you to see if the ideas flow logically. You may need to move your paragraphs about here and look at the way you link them.
- How close is your second draft to the word limit?

ACTIVITY 12 Revise and fine tune

Go through these points and amend your work as necessary.

Congratulations, you are now ready to proof-read your work.

Essential checklist before submission of any written work

This section assumes you have followed the guidance throughout this chapter and have presented the essay in the form of an argument which answers the question in a way that is supported by evidence. Even so, it is essential that you leave time, and make the effort, to proof-read your work before handing it in. Before a final proof-reading, use your word-processing package's spellcheck and grammar-checking facility, ensuring they are set to UK English or as appropriate. Do not blindly accept their recommendations; these packages are not infallible or always suitable for academic writing, so use your judgement. Proof-reading can improve your mark significantly, moving your work into the next grade boundary. Do not attempt to proof-read on screen; print off a copy of your work.

- Is the essay written in a proper academic style?
- Is it well presented in the format requested by the tutor, for example, double line spacing, and wide margins?
- Does every sentence make sense?
- Have you used your secondary sources properly?
- Have you kept to the word limit?
- Are your references and bibliography in the appropriate format?

Learning from feedback

Writing your first essay is a major achievement, and we hope you have learned from the advice in this chapter. There is no expectation that your work will be perfect, whatever that means. If you would like further help with essay writing then you should contact your academic institution's learning support services. Writing essays and getting feedback from your tutor is the best way of learning your craft. Look at the assessment criteria for your piece of work alongside your tutor's comments. Do not just file your essay away in your folder, but spend time thinking about the feedback. Consider what they have identified as your strengths and also your areas for development. These could be useful additions to your Personal Development Plan. Identify any errors relating to grammar and punctuation and try to understand their correction.

Writing reports and dissertations

Much of what has been written above applies to a wide range of other writing you will have to do for your degree. However, if your degree encompasses both vocational and academic learning, it is likely at some stage that you will have to write a report. Reports are a common method of conveying information in the business world and are a regular part of work-based documentation. The most effective reports are those that have clear objectives, concise but precise and balanced arguments and reasoned conclusions.

Structures for reports vary, and you need to seek guidance from your tutor or manager if they have any preferences. However, many reports have the following sections:

- front sheet with, as a minimum, the report title, author and date;
- contents page listing all the main headings together with their page numbers; you may be able to produce a list of contents electronically using your word-processing package;
- summary or abstract covering the main findings, conclusions and recommendations, usually on one side of A4;
- introduction to give a clear statement of purpose;
- background setting the report in context;
- methodology outlining how the investigation was undertaken. What primary and secondary research has been conducted?
- findings should be presented in a logical sequence, moving from the descriptive to the analytical. Directly relevant figures and tables should be included here, background material should go in the appendices;
- conclusions should pick up the themes introduced in the introduction and show what has been established. No new information should be included here;
- recommendations for further action should be identified, these should follow in a logical sequence;
- appendices should contain any directly relevant background material, for example a copy of the questionnaire used to collect the data, together with a list of abbreviations and acronyms if their use has been extensive;
- bibliography should contain books, articles, internet and other sources that have been used to compile the report.

Writing a dissertation or research report

Some degrees require a dissertation or project to be produced, often as a final piece of work. This is a valuable test of your ability to carry out a major piece of research. The academic writing techniques described earlier in this chapter will contribute to your success. Detailed guidance is beyond the scope of this book, although you will find useful techniques for data gathering in chapters 5 and 6. You may need to add the following sections to your report.

After the introduction you could add:

- literature review, findings from existing literature, the sources you used;
- aims of the study, what you are setting out to explore;
- limitations; all research is subject to constraints, what are yours? These may include time and money.

After the findings you could add:

- discussion, this should be a reasoned argument, drawing on primary and secondary research.

After recommendations:

- implications for future research in the field.

If your degree includes the production of a dissertation we suggest you look at the books in the References and further reading sections of this book for guidance.

References and further reading

www.britsoc.co.uk/equality – for British Sociological Association's Guidelines on non-discriminatory language.

Burchfield, H.W. (2004) *The New Fowler's Modern English Usage*, Oxford: Oxford University Press.

King, G. (2004) *Collins Good Punctuation Guide*, Glasgow: HarperCollins.

Lashley, C. and Best, W. (2001) *12 Steps to Study Success*, London and New York: Continuum, pp. 175–202 provide a clear introduction to what is required in writing a dissertation.

www.qaa.ac.uk/academicinfrastructure/FHEQ

Quality Assurance Agency (2001) *The Framework for Higher Education Qualifications*, Gloucester: QAA.

Trask, R.L. (2000) *The Penguin Dictionary of English Grammar*, London: Penguin.

Trask, R.L. (1997) *The Penguin Guide to Punctuation*, London: Penguin.

Truss, L. (2003) *Eats, Shoots & Leaves: the zero tolerance approach to punctuation*, London: Profile Books.

White, B. (2003) *Dissertation Skills for Business and Management Students*, London: Thomson Learning.

9 Developing oral presentation skills

There are few people who can actually say they enjoy making presentations. It is probably one of the greatest causes of anxiety for new students. However, you should take heart, there are many well-known presenters and actors who claim they suffer dreadfully before going in front of an audience, but the adrenaline produced as a result of the stress enables them to give their best performance. Oral presentation is a skill which is worth developing, and will be of use throughout your life in one way or another. During your studies it is essential you find your voice; asking questions, giving opinions in discussion and responding are all ways in which you demonstrate and add to your growing understanding of your subject.

This chapter includes:

- why develop presentation skills?
- participating in seminars and tutorials
- how to plan an effective presentation
- using audio visual aids
- using PowerPoint® and other technology
- making your presentation
- group presentations.

Why develop presentation skills?

Knowing how to make a presentation is a useful skill. You only have to consider the times during your adult life where you might be required to give voice: speaking up at a local planning meeting; voicing your concerns at a parents' evening; making a presentation as part of a job interview; presenting your work at conferences; trying to persuade clients. The list is endless, we are sure you could add more. Effective oral presentation skills cannot be taught; this chapter aims to give you some useful advice, and the rest is up to you. Practice may not make perfect but will certainly make you more confident.

Making a presentation as part of your studies is a good way to consolidate your learning; not only do you have to research your topic but you must understand it as well. It is also a good way to demonstrate your learning; this enables your tutor to assess your knowledge and helps other students to learn. For some of you a presentation allows you to demonstrate knowledge through a wider range of skills. This is particularly advantageous if you find academic writing difficult.

There are a number of different ways you might be asked to make a presentation of your studies and each serves a different purpose. Your presentation may take between 5 and 15 minutes followed by a discussion where others are able to ask questions about your work. Usually, only very experienced speakers are expected to talk for more than 20 minutes. Broadly speaking, presentations are often part of the assessment process. Your presentation may be formally assessed by your tutor and given a mark or grade or assessed informally. In these cases you will most likely be given a verbal or written feedback on your performance and fellow students may also be called on to make an informal assessment; all of which should give you useful pointers for improvement. If no assessment is made of your presentation it makes sense to ask for feedback. The following can all be considered as types of presentation:

- answering questions in a lecture, seminar or discussion group;
- rapporteur in group presentations, discussion groups, meetings;
- tutorial or personal interview;
- chairing a meeting;
- giving an extended response such as a viva or oral examination;
- presentation of a given topic as part of a taught session, either prepared in advance or unseen;
- group presentation;
- giving a paper or seminar presentation;
- presenting a paper at a conference (internal or external);
- explaining or demonstrating a process or product.

The Brunel University website identified that each of these forms of presentation will help to develop the skills listed below, whether you are the speaker or a member of the audience:

- listening
- negotiation
- leadership
- teamwork
- oral communication
- sharing knowledge
- time management
- developing an argument
- collaborating with others from different cultures
- dealing with conflicting opinions
- producing and using visual aids.

Participating in seminars and tutorials

In higher education most lecture sessions will be complemented by seminars. They are an excellent place in which to start to find your voice. Before you can be confident in expressing your ideas you will need to be clear about what you have learned and understood. Putting your thoughts into words is a good way of clarifying your thinking.

The format of seminars varies according to institutional traditions or tutor decisions. The purpose of seminars is to consolidate and add to previous learning, by sharing and developing ideas and considering multiple viewpoints. They are also an excellent way in which to clarify any misunderstandings and become familiar with the particular jargon of your subject.

You may be required to present a previously prepared paper on a given topic, which is then argued and discussed by the group. In this case the tutor takes backstage, acting as a facilitator. Your aim will be to present your ideas clearly and simply. It is not a good idea to read a paper or give a lecture because ideas you might write in a text may be too complex for your audience to absorb. If your purpose is to stimulate a discussion, it is not a good idea to draw conclusions but rather to take a provocative view or ask, but not answer, some leading questions. In this way your audience will be ready to respond with their views based on their understanding of your points and those raised by other study of the topic.

Your audience should have been advised that the point of a seminar is not the destruction of your ideas, it is not a contest. It is the opportunity to share, extend or even offer alternative thoughts and thus extend the learning of all. You should never feel under attack, nor should you behave defensively. The more comfortable you all feel with one another, the more confident you will feel, and the discussions will begin to resemble the thinking in the texts you have been reading.

How to plan an effective presentation

To make your presentation successful four preparatory stages are essential:

1. **Context:** Understanding your audience and the requirements of your presentation
2. **Content:** Researching the topic
3. **Construction:** Writing and organising the presentation
4. **Cross-checking:** Making sure all runs smoothly.

Context – who is listening and what do they want to know?

Before you can present your work it makes sense to think about who you are presenting to and why. Clearly there is a big difference in presenting your ideas to fellow students in a seminar session and presenting a paper at an international conference. Fellow students will not require the same depth and volume of information as examiners who are very familiar with the topic and are assessing your knowledge. An international audience may require depth and breadth of content. You may also have to be much more careful about subject specific language and cultural difference than for an English-speaking audience. However, the underlying principles are the same. Given that you have probably had considerable experience as a member of an audience, as a pupil or as an adult, putting yourself in the audience's shoes should not be too difficult.

ACTIVITY 1 Good and bad

Think of a presentation you have attended. This could be a lecture given by one of your teachers in the past, an address at a public meeting or a presentation by one of your fellow students.

- List the qualities you consider make a good lecture or presentation.
- Now list the poor qualities.

Keep these notes and refer to them when you are planning your presentation.

Answers to the following questions should help you to decide the format of your presentation and how difficult to make it:

- Who are the members of your audience? Are they fellow students or fellow employees, your employer, your assessors; or is your audience national or international?
- What is their relationship to you?
- How many will there be?
- What are they hoping to gain by attending your session?
- What do they already know?
- What is their particular interest?
- Is there anything in your presentation which could cause offence or embar-rassment to members of your audience? How will you deal with that?

If you do not think about these issues your presentation could be:

- too difficult to understand;
- too simple and waste your audience's time;
- offensive to some because you either ignore their values or fail to recognise their expertise and experience;
- boring because it is not appropriate to their needs;
- patronising because you are making assumptions about their lack of knowledge.

If your presentation falls into one or more of these categories you risk alien-ating the people you are addressing. Keeping them on your side is essential, as there is nothing more likely to cause you difficulty or distress than a hostile audience.

Context – understanding the parameters

Where?

Before you can really get started you need to know where you are giving the presentation. Are you following on from someone or will you have to ensure the room is ready? How large is the room? Will this make a difference to the visual aspect of your presentation? Will you have a large or small audience? This could make a significant difference to the type of presentation as, generally, the larger the audience the less interactive the presentation. If you are presenting at a conference you may not be able to check until you arrive.

When?

This may seem a strange question, but there is nothing worse than making extensive preparations only to discover you have the date or time wrong. Another reason for checking the time of your presentation is that audiences often vary according to the time of day. They are usually quite alert and ready to question during the early part of the morning. After lunch they are quite often more sleepy and you may need to take a much livelier approach to keep their attention.

What?

What audio visual aids are there, and who will make sure they available and working when you need them? Do you have other requirements such as darkening facilities in the room? Whose responsibility is it to ensure what you need is available? Are you expected to provide additional information such as handouts? Whose responsibility is it to reproduce them? Consider if you need permission to photocopy your handouts, and whether there any copyright laws pertaining to your material.

How long?

How long is your presentation supposed to last? This is a very important question to answer. Organising your presentation so that it is exactly the correct length is essential. In many situations you will not be allowed to exceed the time; you may be warned shortly before your due time and then stopped, whether you are finished or not. This can be very frustrating. If you end up rushing your conclusions and leave little time for the audience to ask questions, or to engage with your work, and you will lose a golden opportunity to extend your thinking. The answers to these questions will determine the way you plan your presentation.

Content – researching the topic

Researching your topic is essential; whether you chose the topic or not makes no difference. Ask yourself what you would want to know about the topic. Make a 'concept map' and with the topic title in the centre of your page think as broadly as you can. Now organise the ideas into groups. You might need to lose ones that really do not fit in. Now find as much information as you can about each broad heading. You should find that most of the information you require is in those carefully organised notes you have taken during seminars, lectures or about your reading. If the topic is less familiar, you will most certainly have been given clues as to where to look for your information. There is a range of sources you can use; make sure they are up-to-date and accurate and you understand the bias if there is one. As previously mentioned it is not wise to use web sources to support your point unless you have cross-checked and authenticated the information. Note the bibliographic details so that you can acknowledge the sources.

Construction – writing and organising the presentation

If your information gathering has been thorough you will have far too much for a presentation. This is where you distil what you have collected, remembering that too much information will confuse your audience and also be very difficult to present in the time available. Write yourself a rough plan considering the points below:

- Decide what the main argument is.
- Select four or five key points which you can expand on. In shorter presentations you may only manage three.
- Decide what can be left out. For instance, providing contextual details may be essential to aid understanding, if not, omit them.
- Decide what must be left in to help understanding: this may be a brief overview of the project you are basing your talk on.
- Consider if some of your information could be presented as handouts.
- Identify your conclusion.
- Put your points in a logical order: a clear structure will be easier for your audience and you to follow.
- Consider whether visuals or examples would make it easier to understand.

The simple maxim for structuring your presentation referred to in many articles is this:

Tell them what you are going to tell them.

Tell them.

Tell them what you told them.

Make sure that your presentation includes:

- a title that gives your audience a clear idea of what the presentation is about;
- the introduction where you outline what you will cover, giving the aims and objectives and describing briefly how it is structured;
- brief contextual details if necessary;
- the main body of the presentation where you expand on all the areas you identified in the introduction. The points can be structured sequentially or in order of interest. It is usual to start with the most interesting or controversial to catch the attention of the audience. In the main body you:
  - explain complex terms and refer to supporting theories in order to give clarity;
  - provide evidence to support and expand your arguments;
  - give authority to your work by making connections between your work and that of others;
- the conclusion where you summarise the key points you have made.

Cross-checking

Once you have made your plan read it through again, removing anything which is superfluous; even if it is interesting not everything will fit into the time allowed. Think about your plan in terms of the time allocated.

For example if you have 20 minutes:

Introduction – 4 mins

Point 1 – 4 mins

Point 2 – 4 mins

Point 3 – 4 mins

Conclusion – 4 mins

It is only when you start thinking in terms of minutes in which to speak, you realise how little can be said. Therefore it is important to be succinct and to be clear about what is necessary. Obviously your timings can be changed. You may decide to save time on the introduction and conclusion and allocate extra time to the main body. Whatever you do the time must add up.

Ask yourself if you have included anything which you are not sure about. You have a hard decision to make here. It might be you want to impress, but it will almost certainly be an area your audience will want to probe during question time. Can you cope without showing your ignorance and losing face? Can you get additional information in time so you are sure? If not, delete it.

Using audio-visual aids

You now have to decide how this information is going to be presented. Some really accomplished presenters manage without any visual aids, but although they take time to prepare there are numerous arguments in their favour. Although the percentages vary there are sound claims that the significant proportion of what we assimilate is from what we see. Additionally, audio visual aids:

- prevent the audience from being distracted by other visual stimuli;
- help the audience understand concepts (charts and diagrams);
- help the audience to remember;
- give authenticity by using real images (photographs, artworks, plans);
- give authenticity to data (financial data, quotations, and externally sourced statistics);
- can link complex ideas as a flow through chart;
- can compare information;
- give the audience two ways of absorbing information, visual and auditory;
- can identify key points, summarise, illustrate, define and maintain interest.

Other advantages of using visual aids are:

- they can divert attention away from you; this is an advantage if you are feeling nervous;
- you have a record of your presentation which you may be able to use again;
- they act as an *aide-mémoire* while you are talking;
- you can make handouts from the presentation (particularly if you are using overhead transparencies (OHTs) or PowerPoint)

Your decisions about content and presentation will depend on the answers to your questions about the audience, their needs, the venue and so on. You can see that using audio-visual techniques is highly desirable in a presentation. Within this category lies anything from radio and television through to OHTs, video, DVDs, CDs, computer simulations, online presentations, interactive whiteboards, objects and handouts. No matter what the form, they should be visible and intelligible to all and removed when you have finished with them, as they can be very distracting.

Never use an audio-visual aid for the first time without having tested it, until you are confident that you have covered all eventualities. Even then always have a backup plan; technology can and does let you down for the strangest and most unforeseeable reasons.

Radio and television (including CDs, DVDs and video)

There may be programmes, films or sound recordings which have relevance to your presentation. Short extracts which help to illustrate or make sense of a point you are making are an interesting way of presenting an idea.

Never risk inserting 'live' broadcasts into your presentation; programmes can be rescheduled, cancelled and so on.

Advantages

- gives authenticity to your presentation;
- helps audience to become situated in your presentation more readily;
- maintains attention by providing variety;
- reinforces your points;
- video can be impressive.

Disadvantages

- needs careful organisation;
- dependent on good and reliable equipment;
- needs to be prerecorded and played through computer or audio visual link. These are notoriously difficult to synchronise;
- some need a darkened room which can be soporific, especially after lunch.

Overhead transparencies (OHTs)

Acetate sheets which can be printed on via the computer, photocopied, written on during the presentation or bought commercially were once widely used. Most lecture theatres and teaching rooms have the facility to project transparencies, but as they are becoming less common this should be checked.

Text must be large enough to see at the back of the auditorium, use large writing or Arial 18 point as a minimum. Approximately 36 words per slide are ideal and for a 10-minute presentation 6 + 6 + 6 is a good maxim: six slides, six lines of script, no more than six words in each. Photocopies of newspaper articles, archive material, annotated diagrams and so on are unlikely to be legible, but may serve as an illustration which you can briefly describe. Try to think of graphic ways of displaying information: a pie chart is more visible and easier to decode than a table of figures, for example.

Your audience should be able to understand the visual in about 30 seconds. Check with someone who has not seen your slides before by getting them to look at the visual while you talk, turning it off and asking them a few questions that you would hope they could now answer. Number your transparencies in case you drop them.

Advantages

- easy to create trom texts, most photocopiers and modern computers have the facility to print them;
- can be revealed a part at a time;

- easy and flexible to use. You can write on them at the time (although this is not recommended unless your writing is clear and nerves will not affect you);
- coloured reproductions are good;
- total darkness is not essential;
- less likely to be affected by technological problems, but care is needed to keep them in order.

Disadvantages

- can be seen as 'old-fashioned' and low-tech;
- projector images are relatively poor and can distort images;
- colour can be expensive to reproduce.

Flip charts and whiteboards

Flip charts are large A2 pads of inexpensive white paper which will accept standard markers; thin ones are not sufficiently visible. They are presented on a folding stand. Whiteboards replaced the standard green chalk boards in classrooms. Dry-wipe markers specifically designed for use must be used as others will remain permanently on their surface.

Advantages

- flip charts are easy to prepare in advance;
- both are good for feedback from small group discussions;
- both are good for gradually building your presentation.

Disadvantages

- not suitable for large groups;
- require good, legible handwriting;
- whiteboards are not easy to prepare or hide in advance.

Computer simulations and online presentations

These are previously designed programmes to simulate real life situations. For example the audience may be asked take part in the processes necessary to market a new product. It relies to a large extent on role play. If you want to show a website, you could use screen captures rather than risking going online.

Advantages

- ready-made packages can be downloaded from a range of sources on the internet;

- particularly useful for certain disciplines, such as engineering and business;
- your HE establishment may have a licence;
- graded for different levels of use.

Disadvantages

- not your work so may not be useful if you are being assessed;
- needs a lot of organisation as most are interactive;
- early planning is essential;
- not suitable with large groups;
- audience may not feel comfortable in role.

Interactive whiteboards

There are two types of interactive whiteboards

1. Electronic version of 'dry-wipe' on a computer that allows students in a virtual classroom to see what the instructor, presenter or fellow student writes or draws. This is commonly used in conferencing and data-sharing situations.

2. A large display panel which can be used as a conventional whiteboard, projector screen or computer projector screen. The image can be controlled by touching or writing on the surface with a special pen rather than using the mouse and keyboard. The following is about the latter.

Advantages

- you are completely in control of the data presentation and it is easy to use;
- they are an excellent example of e-learning;
- presentations can be enhanced with pictures and imported tables and texts;
- they are an alternative way for learners to absorb information;
- the audience can take part in discussions or group work as part of the presentation;
- notes can be stored for later use or as part of networked learning.

Disadvantages

- board can be obscured by presenter;
- tend to be more suited to standard classrooms. Size of text and detail must be considered if presenting to large arena. The quality of facilities varies and must be checked;
- multiple data can become jumbled on screen;
- must be planned carefully.

Slide projector transparencies

Photographic slides which are shown on a slide projector. Most universities will have an archive collection of transparencies.

Advantages

- most colourful and authentic means of enhancing presentation especially for artworks or historical data;
- cheap and easy to produce;
- not very commonplace.

Disadvantages

- darkened room essential therefore tend to be shown in batches;
- danger of obscuring screen when pointing out details;
- can become damaged or lost over time;
- projected images can enhance appearance. Reproduced artworks are not always true in colour;
- modern projectors will not accommodate card mounts and archive material frequently needs remounting;
- inaccurately loaded slides are very distracting for you and the audience.

Artefacts

Some presenters will bring examples which are relevant to their talk for the audience to handle. Health and safety risks must be considered. Again, many universities, museums and galleries have a handling collection which can be borrowed.

Advantages

- can add authenticity;
- tangible illustration of part of the presentation such as a model of the heart or cell structure;
- allows audience to learn through the additional senses of touch and possibly smell;
- can be easy to obtain.

Disadvantages

- only suited for small groups as handling is slow and can be disruptive
- time is needed for examination and presentation cannot continue simultaneously;
- precious, potentially dangerous, large or very small objects are not very suitable.

Handouts

Previously prepared and photocopied notes for the audience. These can vary in length and purpose.

Advantages

- reinforces your presentation and allows you to provide additional material you may not have time to present;
- simple to produce from PowerPoint slides;
- audience can use them to annotate during the lecture;
- can be referred to during the presentation;
- gives audience a means of checking at a later time something they may have missed.

Disadvantages

- can be distracting, audience may be reading rather than listening;
- rustling papers can be distracting to you and the audience;
- notes should not be too full or your audience will feel they need not have attended.

Using PowerPoint and other technology

PowerPoint® is becoming one of the most common ways to make a presentation. Unfortunately, it is so widely used that 'death by PowerPoint' has become a real danger and there is a possibility that the audience can 'switch off'. So when you are considering what to use to enhance your presentation, ask yourself if it is the best method for you or might others be as successful.

Many computer software packages come with Microsoft PowerPoint ready loaded. When you click on the PowerPoint icon on your desktop you will be given the option of choosing whether to use the auto content wizard or to devise your own. Unless the options they offer are suited to your needs it makes sense to design your own. It is not difficult, the programme will guide you and with practice you will become proficient. Again, many HE institutions provide courses in using PowerPoint.

As with any technology there is always the risk of problems. It makes sense to print your presentation and make OHP transparencies and handouts and also save it to memory stick, CD or by e-mailing it to an accessible account. You also need to check that your operating system is compatible with the PC or laptop you will use for the presentation, especially if you are using an Apple Mac.

PowerPoint presentations do take time to set up and require plenty of practice. The same rules apply as for OHP presentations, in that legibility is crucial and the 6 + 6 + 6 maxim applies. It is also best to limit gimmicks such as text flying in or crumbling; it can be annoying. Colour is interesting, but remember yellow and orange have a very short focal length and are difficult to see from a distance. As a general rule if you are using text only, white on a blue background or black on a tinted ground are easier on the eye because the text is clearer to read.

Making your presentation

Final checks

Before you can make your presentation there are still a number of things which must be done. Practise, practise, practise. The more familiar you become with your presentation the more confident you will feel. On the other hand, try not to learn it by heart, you will end up reciting it if you are not careful and it could sound very boring. Accept that each time you rehearse you will use slightly different phrasing; this is good because it indicates that you are becoming so familiar with your presentation you can talk with ease.

Case Study Heather says: 'Practice and more practice, find a friend who can give constructive criticism and advice.' Dianne advises: 'read aloud to yourself in front of a mirror or a small audience.'

You may become so familiar with your presentation that you feel you can give it without notes, however prompts are a good idea; nerves have a nasty habit of clearing the mind of anything useful. Prepare your presentation notes so that they give you enough support, are visible (even in subdued lighting), and have all visuals such as slides or PowerPoint frames identified at the point in the presentation when you want to refer to them. You will in the end devise your own method but here are three suggestions for good delivery:

- simplify your presentation, highlight or embolden the key points and print in 14 or 16 point Arial;
- have cue cards with key points matching each visual. Number the cards or hold them together with a treasury tag;
- prepare your slides in such a way that each acts as a prompt.

Read your presentation aloud, using your visual aids at the same time. You could use a tape recorder and listen for hesitation, indistinct words or repeated phrases. Time yourself, remember you need to speak more slowly than usual, between 130 and 150 words per minute is recommended. This enables your audience to take in what you are saying and make notes without losing the thread. Take time to breathe between each point. If you exceed the time allowed decide what you can prune to make your material fit. Most people prepare far too much.

Check your visuals for spelling mistakes, get someone else to read them as errors are easily overlooked and spellchecker will not find everything.

The presentation

Giving a presentation is a performance; acknowledge that you are nervous but try not to let the audience know. A little tension is good, because it ensures we perform well, but too much can produce miserable side-effects.

> **Case Study** LisaMarie: says 'You will feel nervous, but try not to panic. Everyone feels nervous when they have to speak in public. Try not to get into a state.' Julie says: 'Be well prepared and treat it as a learning experience. It is something that everyone worries about so learn by watching your peers.'

So what can you do? Clearly practice is the most important solution, but there are also other ways to tame your fears. Think of what is scaring you and then think of strategies that will help. Then imagine the very worst things that could happen, even if you give a really bad presentation. Giving voice to our fears does help to get them into perspective.

> **Case Study** As Jason says: 'The anticipation is always worse than the actual task. Volunteer to go first!'

Rudd (2004) suggests useful relaxation techniques; deep breathing helps to reduce the effects of the adrenalin rushing around your body and can slow the heartbeat. Exercise also has the same effect. Whatever you do, alcohol is not a good idea nor are other relaxants; they can make you sleepy or too laid back. Reward yourself afterwards if you want to.

Hints Pointers for success

- Be confident, you know more than your audience on this particular topic.
- Respect your audience, establish eye contact and smile. Remember, body language says a lot about you, stand up straight, slouching suggests you are not interested. Use hand and body gestures to illustrate points. Ffion suggests that you 'look at the audience, smile and speak loudly and clearly. Hold yourself confidently, subconsciously your audience will be drawn to listen to you.'
- Speak clearly and sound enthusiastic and interested.
- Try not to create barriers between you and your audience. Standing behind your equipment, masking or touching your face with your hand, sitting relaxed

▶

or cross-legged or fiddling with jewellery, loose change and so on can all create an impression of lack of interest.

- Introduce yourself and give the title and brief outline of your presentation.
- Use 'signposts'; these give the audience an idea of what to expect, and this helps them to move with you through the presentation. Use phrases such as 'Now we will consider the effect', 'We have just thought about the key recommendations, now let's consider their implementation'.
- To engage your audience you could ask questions, change the tone of your voice, add quotations or cite evidence.
- If you are using visual aids remember not to stand in front of the screen, use a pointer if possible and project your words to the audience.
- Be aware of the time. A watch prominently placed helps. Be prepared to leave some things out if necessary but make sure you leave time for questions.
- If questions are slow to come, look encouragingly at your audience.
  - listen carefully to questioners to ensure you understand, if necessary repeating it so that the whole audience can hear
  - rephrase a difficult question so that your understanding is checked
  - speak to the whole audience as it is never a good idea to enter into a dialogue with the questioner; your audience will feel excluded
  - do not take what appear to be hostile or argumentative questions personally
  - if you cannot answer a question do not be afraid to say so. State that you will get back to them later with an answer
  - if a question is inappropriate suggest you could talk to the questioner afterwards.

Group presentations

Group presentations are often used by tutors as a means of assessing your knowledge and understanding, as well as your ability to work as part of a team. They are an efficient use of time and give variety to the sessions. Many students prefer this way of taking the limelight as the anxiety is shared. The presentation will take one of two forms:

- **Seen:** where the topic has been given beforehand and there is time to prepare in advance.
- **Unseen:** where the topic, or maybe a paper to read, is given to the group. Time is allowed before they give a summary of their understanding to other students in the seminar or lecture.

In both cases the same principles apply:

- all need to have reached an agreement about the requirements of the task;
- roles and responsibilities should be agreed;
- a spokesperson or leader needs to be appointed.

With group presentations there is a greater risk of overlooking details, particularly those of organisation. It makes sense to build in enough planning time, have agreed time limits when tasks will be completed, appoint someone to check final details and have a contingency plan for unexpected absence.

When working as a team it is important that all participants are aware of the psychology of group work and group dynamics and recognise that most groups will contain those who:

- wish to lead and find it difficult to accept other views;
- will seek to present themselves in the best light, maybe at the expense of others;
- are willing to contribute but can be disruptive if overlooked;
- need to be encouraged to participate but will remain passive if not, and can be overlooked;
- agree to accept a responsibility but are unreliable;
- will do almost anything to avoid taking part or making a contribution.

The longer a group has to prepare the more likely the group dynamic moves to a second phase where leaders are challenged and individuals break away.

Wherever you see yourself in this hierarchy it is important to remember that with group presentations you are part of a team and therefore your individual wants and needs come second to the shared and agreed ideas of the group. The advantages of working collaboratively as a group outweigh the disadvantages. Sharing your ideas and knowledge enables you to extend and verify your own thinking.

As stated at the beginning of the chapter, learning how to make a presentation, whether it is to a seminar group, a team at work or a larger audience at a conference, is a skill which improves with practice. This skill will be honed by constructive criticism and has numerous applications for life. Do not expect to enjoy the anticipation or preparation, but look forward to the sense of relief and achievement once the presentation is over.

References and further reading

www.brunel.ac.uk/learnhigher/participating-in-seminars – for helpful training videos and a comprehensive list of other websites where more information and self-help advice can be found.

www.open.ac.uk/inclusiveteaching/pages/inclusive-teaching/discussions-groupwork-and-presentations.php

www.rdg.ac.uk/studyskills

Rudd, D. (2004) *Giving a presentation* – available from http://data.bolton.ac.uk/learning/helpguides/studyskills/present.pdf.

www.worcester.ac.uk/studyskills

10 Coping with exams and revision

Many students feel that the difficulties of combining work and study and balancing the demands of friends and family contribute to a feeling of stress. This is particularly the case at exam time. We will look specifically at how you can prepare for examinations, through effective revision and good exam technique. We will share with you some lessons from our students, to enable you to devise a workable revision plan that meets your needs, allows you to cope with pressure and stress, and maximises your chances of success.

This chapter covers:

- stress management
- drawing up your revision timetable
- important preparation before the exam
- techniques for exam success.

Stress management

Not all stress is bad. We do need some stress in our lives to help to get things done. We each function best and feel best at our own optimal level of physiological arousal. Too little can lead to boredom, but too much can produce feelings of worry or panic and problems seem insurmountable. Often this is a gradual process that you do not notice until it begins to affect you physically, mentally and emotionally.

As already mentioned in the first chapter, organising your time is one of the best ways to reduce stress, but here are some other suggestions you may like to consider:

- Look after your diet, so do not drink too much coffee, tea and fizzy drinks; the caffeine will dehydrate you and make your thinking less clear. Drink plenty of water and eat healthily and regularly; your brain will benefit from the nutrients. Some people like to take a multivitamin tablet to help them through particularly stressful periods.
- Regular moderate exercise will boost your energy, clear your mind and reduce any feelings of stress.
- Try out some yoga, tai chi or relaxation techniques. Experiment until you find something that works for you; it could be as simple as a long

bath or listening to some music. You will find that it will help to keep you feeling calm and balanced, improve your concentration levels and you should sleep better.

- Exercise some self-belief. You were given a place on the course because people believed you have the ability to succeed.
- It is unrealistic to expect to be perfect. You should aim to do what you can, but keep things in perspective.

Sometimes you may find that you are overwhelmed; this is a time when many students decide to discontinue their studies. It is important to take action. Avoiding the issue will not make the problem go away, and may often make it worse. It is important to ask for help from your lecturer or personal tutor as early as possible. Do remember that some staff may only have limited time to help you. Before you ask for a meeting, ensure that you have done as much as possible to resolve the issue yourself.

If you are feeling so anxious that you are experiencing difficulties in sleeping and your health is suffering, or your relationships with other people are starting to be affected, then it is important to seek some professional help. You should have been given information about these services during your induction. They are there to help you and will, in most cases, offer free and confidential support. Consider the following advice:

- **Relax:** stress reduces your ability to learn. Take deep breaths and relax your shoulders before starting to learn, formally or informally.
- **Remember:** all the good experiences that made you feel proud, the birth of a child, a sporting achievement and so on.
- **Replenish:** a balanced diet keeps your brain in top gear. Proteins and plenty of water help the memory. Carbohydrates tend to make us sluggish.
- **Absorb:** remember how you prefer to learn and be positive. We are often as successful as we expect to be; above all, enjoy.

Case Study Frances offers the following reassurance:

'There is a lot of pressure around exam times, given that it is over 30 years since I sat an exam. Revision dominated everything, but it was as much about the exam technique as the knowledge required.'

Drawing up your revision timetable

One of the most common pressure points is the period leading up to examinations. So we will focus on how to reduce anxiety by effective revision and exam technique. From the time management tips in chapter 1 you will understand the need to leave plenty of time to revise, so that you do not get into a situation of having to do last-minute cramming. It may also be helpful to book some time off work. A timetable can motivate you and provide confidence as you complete each topic. It is a good idea to start at least six weeks before your examination, and up to two months ahead if you feel particularly anxious.

> **Case Study** Carol suggests you 'start early to avoid any unexpected complications; it always takes longer than you think.'

You need to think about the following issues in order to draw up your revision timetable:

- What are your examination start and end dates? Work your way backwards from the exam date to cover each topic appropriately before the due date.
- Try to ensure you do something for each topic each week. Even just summarising your notes will keep the main subject ideas fresh in your mind.
- Are you going to work with other people? If so you need to check their availability.
- How do you work most effectively? If you do your work best first thing in the morning then allocate slots as appropriate. Also consider if you are more effective with short intensive sessions of less than an hour, or whole blocks of time such as an evening.
- Make sure you balance the time you have available between the subjects, not neglecting ones you find particularly easy or difficult.
- Which topics are you going to revise? It is unlikely that you will be able to revise everything, so you need to make some careful decisions based on past papers, course content and your own particular areas of interest.
- As you use your timetable, make sure you monitor your progress, perhaps using highlighter pens as a visual indication of how much you have completed. Do not forget to reward yourself when you complete a topic or at other key points. It may be helpful to compare draft revision timetables with other students to see how they differ.

> **Case Study** Marilyn suggests you 'focus, start early – an hour of two of work a day really helps. Manage your day, if work has been dreadful then give yourself a night off.'

ACTIVITY 1 Plan your timetable

Now draw up your revision timetable for at least six weeks before the exams are due to start. Start by noting essential non-study commitments such as employment and important social or family dates. You may need to confirm work, childcare and other arrangements for the exam period. Then allocate topics to days, but do build in some flexibility.

The most effective way to revise is to really engage with and understand what you have learned. You will get very little from the process of reading and re-reading your notes. It is a good idea to experiment with several alternative revision techniques so that it is more fun and your motivation to study is high. Here are some ideas for you to consider:

- Look closely at the assessment criteria for each of the subjects; this will tell you the standard your answers must be for each grade.
- Summarise your course materials onto index cards, thinking about appropriate headings. Look at the learning objectives published in the course handbook. Identify definitions, concepts, key points and examples for each topic, then gradually reduce the number of cards you use. Eventually you will only have a few cards each containing the most important information. Test yourself on these.

> **Case Study** Rob describes this technique: 'It involved distilling ever more summarised versions of my notes onto index cards. By memorising the index cards I found I could build each topic back up when required, and apply the relevant information to the exam question.'

- Try a wide range of memory strategies, use mind maps, diagrams or flowcharts, experiment with shapes and colour and make poster displays, make up mnemonics for key facts, write out key ideas on Post-it notes and distribute around your house. For further ideas have a look at Tony Buzan's short book, *Brilliant Memory: unlock the power of your mind*.
- Work with others from your degree course to form a 'revision club'. Here each of you tackle and present a particular theory or area of knowledge to the rest of your group, even devising possible exam questions for others to answer.

> **Case Study** Susan said: 'I found having a "study buddy" invaluable. We used to meet up a couple of times a week, bounce ideas off each other and verbally answer the questions. I found this such a positive learning experience.' Frances said: 'A small number of us used to meet to have a coffee, compare notes and generally support each other through the inevitable lows. This support group became essential at exam revision times. We met the weekend before the exam to stimulate our brains through constant conversation, question asking, exchanging ideas and views. It really helped to get "into the zone".'

- Always work through questions from past papers if they are available, if possible listing a series of past questions for each area revised. After revising a topic, answer a question on it, and then compare your answer to your notes. If you are short of time then an outline plan or a mindmap will do. If you can swap your answers with fellow students they may give you valuable feedback. Also look at model answers if they are available.

■ As you get nearer to the exam date it is essential to practise writing answers in the time allocated. It is important that you practise writing quickly and neatly in longhand, as writing for three hours without a computer is a skill you may need to develop.

ACTIVITY 2 Take a practice exam

Choose an examination paper you have not studied closely and answer the appropriate number of questions for the full exam. Work in a quiet place and do not take breaks. If possible give your answers to a fellow student to mark.

Important preparation before the exam

Planning an examination strategy

At an early stage in your revision there is certain key information you require so you can maximise your performance. Make sure you can answer the questions below for each examination you take.

ACTIVITY 3 Identify the key information

Make sure you consider the questions below:

■ Is the paper divided into sections?

■ How many questions are you expected to answer?

■ Are there any specific instructions about question choice?

■ What is the nature of the questions – essays, seen papers, short answer, multiple choice, case studies?

■ What proportion of marks is allocated to each section or question?

■ How long is the exam? Convert this time into minutes.

■ Now allocate, say, 5 per cent of the total minutes for choosing your questions and 10 per cent for final proof-reading.

■ Divide the remaining 85 per cent of time across the questions according to their weighting and so arrive at an ideal time per answer.

■ Make out a schedule of this information from the start time to the finish of the exam and try and memorise this.

■ Think about the balance of time that you will dedicate to planning and writing each answer.

The night before the exam

It really is counterproductive to try and cram in facts the night before an exam as this just leads to fatigue. Remind yourself that you have followed a revision programme and have done your best.

Case Study	Cally advises: 'Don't cram, give yourself a bit of time off. It works. Marathon runners don't run a practice marathon the day before a major event, so why expect your brain to work better if you burn the midnight oil.'

Then follow the tips below:

- Get your clothes and equipment ready. See the checklist below.
- Have a bath to relax, and avoid drinking caffeine or alcohol.
- Double-check your alarm clock, giving yourself plenty of time to get to the exam. Plan to leave much earlier than normal, to take account of any transport delays.
- Watch something distracting on television or read something light. Then go to bed at a reasonable time and try to rest.

Checklist of things to take to the examination room

ID card or other identity information

Writing kit, this could include pens and pencils (plus spares), highlighters, ruler, eraser and correction fluid if permitted

Specialist equipment permitted such as calculators (with spare batteries), mathematical equipment

Texts for open book examinations and a dictionary, if allowed

Bottle of water

Watch or clock for timekeeping (although there will be clocks prominently displayed and the invigilators may mark off time remaining on a board).

The day of the exam

It is normal to feel nervous but do try to relax so you are able to perform as well as possible. Here are some ideas to help you:

- Have something to eat before leaving home.
- Check exactly where the exam room is, and what time you are required. Then get some quiet time by yourself. Remind yourself that you have worked steadily in the time leading up to the exam, and that you will have done the best you can, whatever the outcome.

- Avoid last-minute revision as this may leave you feeling muddled and anxious.
- Avoid conversations with others just before the exam, you need to keep focused and positive.
- Follow instructions about what you may and may not take into the exam room. Be particularly aware of the rules regarding mobile phones. These are often banned completely from examination rooms.
- If the desks are numbered make sure you are sitting in the correct place.

Techniques for exam success

Select the best questions for you

- Read the instructions on the front of the paper carefully, and check that the questions are arranged as expected.
- Read all the questions slowly and carefully. Highlight key words and make sure you understand exactly what you are being asked to do. Check there are no questions you have missed on the back of the exam paper.
- Decide which questions you are going to answer and then answer your best question first, as this will help you to feel calm and confident.
- Always plan your longer answers or essay questions before you start writing, and ensure that your plan covers all aspects of the question and is weighted appropriately. However, do not spend too long planning, produce an outline and then start writing.
- Provide definitions of key terms and appropriate evidence, and remember to analyse and evaluate rather than merely describe.
- Where appropriate, include references to theory, although you will probably not be expected to produce a list of references or a bibliography unless you are taking an open book examination.

Time management for examinations

- As soon as you are allowed to write, note down the start and finish time of each question as identified in your strategy. Allow a few minutes at the start to read through and decide which questions to answer and in which order and allow time at the end to proof-read your answers.
- Always move on to the next question at the end of the time you have allocated yourself, rather than try to produce a 'perfect' answer. If you do not answer the right number of questions you will make it far less easy to obtain a pass grade.

> **Case Study** Don says: 'I carved up the time I had into planning and writing time, and stuck to it. If I hadn't finished a question I still moved on. There are more marks available for answering every question moderately well than for providing fantastic answers to a small proportion of them.'

- If you run out of time for a particular question, or you get really stuck, move on and do not panic. But do leave sufficient space on your paper, so that you can add in points later if there is time. You may find ideas come to you when you are working on something else, in which case make some notes at the back of your examination paper or on your essay plan. These can be struck through before you give in your paper.

Presentation of your answers

- Write as clearly and neatly as you can so the examiner finds your work easy to mark. If, when you are checking your work, you find you have missed out a word or wish to add in or strengthen a point, then add it neatly into the text or as a footnote at the bottom of the page.

Dealing with exam anxiety

- If you do begin to panic at any time during the exam, try closing your eyes and taking several slow, deep breaths to calm down your nervous system. Some people like to focus on positive thoughts – 'I can pass this exam', 'I am well prepared', 'I am calm' – while doing this deep breathing.

Review all your answers to maximise marks

- Always take time at the end of the examination to review your work, reading through for spelling, grammar and sense (and to check your name or identify number is on the paper).
- Ask yourself if you have really answered the questions set and, if necessary, add extra material clearly indicating where it should be inserted into the text.

> **Case Study** Lorraine comments: 'If the examiner asks for three examples, don't give five hoping they'll mark the best three. Put your efforts into making the three examples really good.'

And finally, after the exam try and avoid post-mortem discussions with other students if you are feeling anxious about your performance. Just tell yourself you've done the best you can at this stage and then move on.

Case Study	Jenny, who had to retake some exams, confirms: 'It can be done. I am proof. I was determined not to be defeatist and told myself I would get there in the end. I've found the exams extremely hard, but the overwhelming sense of achievement I know I'll feel when I finally graduate keeps me going.'

Reference and further reading

Buzan, T. (2006) *Brilliant Memory: unlock the power of your mind*, Harlow: BBC Active.

11 After your degree: looking to the future

This final chapter has a particular focus on what you are going to do next. This could be progression to a higher degree or professional qualifications, applying for a new job, or considering other opportunities ahead. It builds on the personal development plan you produced in chapter 2. We will discuss how to produce a generic curriculum vitae (CV) which you can update for each application you make. You may want to come back to these sections at appropriate times in the future. Our aim is to give you some pointers for your personal and career development.

This chapter covers:

- using your careers service
- auditing your experiences
- writing a professional CV
- completing your application.

Using your careers service

Every educational institution will have a careers advisory service and you should tap into their wealth of professional expertise. This book has been written on the basis that you are studying and are likely to be already employed. However, by completing your degree, you will have opened up a wide range of further opportunities. Your HE careers service can help to point you in the right direction; whether it is towards further academic or professional study; a first step on the ladder to a new career; making a sideways move; or gaining a promotion.

Case Study Julie says: 'My degree has opened many doors for me, I now feel I have a choice. I intend to continue to study as I'm hooked!'

ACTIVITY 1 Contact Careers Advisory Service (CAS)

Find out the contact details of your careers advisory service. If you are currently studying for your degree at a college of further education, you may be enrolled as both a student of the college and the university. If this is the case, you should initially investigate both services, although the university HE advisory service may be more appropriate to your needs. Make an appointment to discuss your future plans.

By studying for your degree you will have demonstrated many personal and academic skills. If you have undertaken personal development planning (PDP) as part of your degree, you will already have a good knowledge of your career-related interests, skills, aptitudes, preferences and goals. This information will be helpful to your careers adviser, and you should take your personal development plan to the first meeting. They will also find the latest copy of your CV helpful. There is advice on how to prepare a CV later in this chapter. You should complete a draft version of this before your first meeting.

It is also important that you are able to identify, understand and articulate any limitations that may affect your plans.

ACTIVITY 2 Consider constraints

Think about any barriers to learning you may have identified at the start of your degree. How many of these now apply? Are there any you need to add to the list? It is important you share any constraints with your careers adviser, so put this list with your personal development plan and your CV ready for your first meeting.

Auditing your experiences

As a successful degree student you will have a great deal to offer future employers. Even if you are currently satisfied at work you should always have a CV written and ready to tailor to opportunities as they arise. We strongly advise you to produce a CV at this stage in your career. It is a good opportunity to reflect on your recent achievements. A CV will also be a useful addition to your professional development portfolio. It could also be a helpful prompt in meetings with admissions staff for higher degrees, current and future employers, and may also help you obtain some freelance work. The next part of the text offers some helpful tips.

Which personal details should you include?

We will divide the preparation and writing of your CV into several sections, and offer our own views on different styles and content. There is no one correct way to produce a CV, so work through each of the sections and then make up your own mind about what to include. Some information will remain static, such as personal details, but other areas will need to be tailored to meet each particular opportunity. However, your personal details will need to be on every copy you send out.

We recommend that every CV has:

- **Your full name, address and telephone number:** we need to issue a word of warning here: if possible you need to be in control of this number, and ensure it is answered professionally. If you give your mobile phone number, remember it can ring at any time. The answer phone message needs to be appropriate;
- **Personal e-mail address:** rather than your work details if you are looking for another job;
- **Nationality:** employers are now required to prove that the person they employ is eligible to work in the European Union. You might want to address this by stating your nationality on your CV. Nevertheless, new employers should ask you to produce your passport or your National Insurance number to prove you are able to work legally, so make sure you can do this.

You may also want to think about:

- **Date of birth, rather than age:** although this should not be relevant, particularly with age discrimination legislation; potential employers will often try and work this out from when you left school;
- **Marital or partnership status:** this is not relevant to any job application, but some of our students say they are proud of their status, and also want to include details of their children's names and ages. Our advice is to limit such personal information to married, in partnership or single at the most.

Gathering information on education, training and other interests

Now is the time to revisit your qualifications and training, and to really promote your degree level qualification. Qualifications should be listed from the most recent first, as long as this does not obscure a really impressive achievement. Start with making a note of the full details of your degree. You might also think about whether you can approach your tutor to act as one of your referees in the future. There is some guidance on approaching referees in the next section.

Now look back at any other qualifications and certificates you may have gained. Ask yourself:

- Did you leave school with qualifications in English and Maths, for example, 'O' level, CSE grade 1, GCSE, key skills stage 2, or have you gained these since?

- What other qualifications did you achieve at school?
- Since leaving school have you gained any other vocational, professional or academic qualifications?

ACTIVITY 3 Qualifications

Gather together any certificates you can find. Many larger employers ask for copies of relevant certificates so you may need to write to the examining bodies for a replacement if you have lost something critical. Draft a list of your qualifications in order showing the level, subject, grade and school/college/university attended. Start with your degree and work backwards. You should edit this list later, perhaps grouping together school qualifications as '4 "O" levels including English and Maths', or 'a good general education', but at this stage it is important to see the whole picture. Some employers' application forms ask for this level of detail so hopefully your efforts to search out the information will not be wasted.

You should also consider any training or development courses you have attended through work, or on your own initiative over the last few years. These activities may indicate an impressive commitment to your own personal development.

Look through these questions to remind yourself of what else you have learned and achieved:

- Are you a member of any professional organisations?
- Do you have a full driving licence?
- Which software and operating systems are you currently using?
- What IT training have you done? Did you gain any certificates? Make a list of IT courses you have attended with their dates and levels.
- Do you have any foreign language skills? If so, which languages and to what level of fluency? Did you gain certificates for these skills?
- Are there any short courses you have attended that you have forgotten about? Look back at any appraisal or staff development records you may have from work to remind you.
- Have you been trained as a First Aider or Appointed Person? Employers are often impressed by this. Even if your certificate has lapsed it may be worth including.
- Have you been trained in counselling or youth work?
- Have you received clearance from the Criminal Records Bureau if you want to work with children or vulnerable adults?
- Do you have any sports or coaching awards?
- Finally, think about your interests, hobbies and any sports you play. List any positions of responsibility you hold or have held in any club or organisation, and state what your achievements were.

ACTIVITY 4 Training

Now draft a section on your training, based on the information you have gathered above. You may have to edit this later, but you should be positive about your accomplishments.

Thinking about your work experience

Once again, our advice would be to start with what you are doing now and to work backwards, as employers are probably more interested in your most recent experience. You do not have to list the full address of your employer on your CV, name and location should be sufficient, but it is worth looking up the full details as sometimes these are requested on application forms. If you have been working for many years it is acceptable to summarise your early employment record. Do not be concerned if, at this stage, you seem to have varied, limited or largely unpaid work experience. We will advise you how best to present this data further on in the chapter. For now let's have a look at what you have gathered so far.

ACTIVITY 5 Employment

Find as much information as possible about your employment over the last few years. Look back and try and put down details for the last ten years or so. In particular, find out:

- the full name, address and telephone number of each of your employers and write a brief description of the service they provide;

- your start date, end date and final salary, together with the total weekly hours you worked if part time. Note, you should not put your salary on your CV, save this for negotiating when you are offered the job;

- job title, did this change over the period of employment?

- summarise your main responsibilities in each post. If you have a copy of your job description this will be helpful. List any particular achievements, and be specific and positive about skills you developed in the job;

- finally, consider if there is a person you can ask to act as a referee, particularly from your more recent employment. Always seek permission first and, if they agree, give them a copy of your CV when it is completed, and keep them in touch with your progress. Find out their correct job title, e-mail and phone number as well as a full contact address. This is vital so your references can be checked.

Depending on your age and experience, you may now have a large file of information, or something very slim if your work experience has been pre-dominantly casual. We are sure that when you look back on what you have done, you will be able to offer a useful set of skills which can be transferred to a work environment. Do not overlook or undervalue any unpaid work experience, it is important to add this to the exercise you completed above. In each case include details of your responsibilities, achievements and skills. You should also include:

- any voluntary work for a charity or community-based scheme;
- any period of self-employment;
- unpaid work experience, perhaps as part of a period of study;
- time when you brought up children or cared for a family member.

Writing a professional CV

By completing the tasks above you have gathered considerable information that we hope will be useful in making future applications, be they for HE, professional memberships or for employment. The more professional your CV is, the more likely you are to make your application stand out positively. This section will take you through the process. Remember, you will need to tailor your CV for each different job opportunity. You should take note of the knowledge, experience, skills and personal attributes suggested in the application details, particularly if a person specification is included for the post.

Chronological or skills-based CV?

There are two standard styles of CV, chronological and skills-based, and examples of the layout of each can be found in Figures 11.1 and 11.2. You are likely to be familiar with the layout of a chronological CV, which lists your jobs and education in most recent date order and is useful for showing steady progress. This style may be less suitable for you if you have changed jobs frequently, or have gaps in your career history. In this case a skills-based CV could be more appropriate. You should consider whether to list your 'Career Achievements' or 'Education and Training' section first. If you have little work experience it is probably best to sell your achievements as a degree student before giving information on casual jobs.

A skills-based CV highlights your skills and achievements rather than your work or education history. This works well if you write it considering the requirements of the position you are applying for, as it makes your transferable skills and qualities immediately clear. It is useful if you wish to change career direction, are not currently in work, or if you have had a break or spells of unemployment. However, some recruiters state they suspect skills-based CVs are used to hide patchy work histories; so be aware of this and write strongly about the work experience you have had, be it paid or less formal. Additionally, describe how you usefully filled the periods of unemployment.

CURRICULUM VITAE

NAME

Address

Telephone number

Email

PROFILE (if using)

CAREER ACHIEVEMENTS

Job title	Company name/location	Dates
(details of responsibilities and achievements here)		

Job title	Company name/location	Dates
(details of responsibilities and achievements here)		

EDUCATION AND TRAINING

Qualification	Institution	Dates

(details of training courses here)

ADDITIONAL INFORMATION

Date of birth	DD/MM/YYYY

References available on request

Figure 11.1 Layout of a chronological CV

The optional personal profile summary

A profile is a summary of what you have to offer, and is usually placed at the top of the CV to attract the attention of the person reading it. It should inform your reader of your aims and what skills you have to offer. List your major skills, strengths, personal qualities and achievements. Be specific, give examples – good team player, excellent written skills, versatile, able to motivate others and so on. Stating your career objective at the outset makes your job aspirations clear, and may encourage the employer to read further. A profile has advantages and disadvantages. A well-written profile that matches the needs of the employer is useful, particularly if you are sending in a speculative CV to a large organisation, and it adds to the information you provide in the CV. Some employers, however, take the view that many profiles are empty hype and, indeed, many are.

CURRICULUM VITAE

NAME

Address

Telephone number

Email

PROFILE (if using)

KEY SKILLS

Title of first skill and description

Title of second skill and description

Title of third skill and description

CAREER SUMMARY

Job title	Company name/location	Dates
Job title	Company name/location	Dates

EDUCATION AND TRAINING

Qualification	Institution	Dates

(details of training courses here)

ADDITIONAL INFORMATION

Date of birth	DD/MM/YYYY

Figure 11:2 Layout of a skills based CV

Now you should write your CV, either using an online form (see Activity 6) or a word processor, as in Activity 7.

ACTIVITY 6 Online CV

If you wish to produce your CV online, you should use a reputable careers advice service such as learndirect (**www.learndirect-advice.co.uk**), which offers general careers advice, or **www.prospects.ac.uk**, the UK's official graduate careers website. For both sites you will need to register. Register following the 'My Prospects' link for this invaluable site for HE students, which provides some excellent guidance on writing CVs, application letters and interview techniques.

By registering with Prospects you will be able to produce up to three online CVs that you can amend whenever you need. If you have graduated you can even have a professional careers consultant check your CV, and give you personal advice on improving its quality and marketability. This is a one-off service, for a small fee, so you should make sure that the CV you submit is your best effort. You will receive written feedback by e-mail in three working days.

ACTIVITY 7 Word-processed CV

Write your CV using a word processing package, with clear section headings. If you use Microsoft Office® you can have a look at its templates and try using the CV wizard.

Some final words of advice

- Do not include photographs unless really relevant. This may be appropriate in limited cases, for example, for jobs in the creative arts such as performance artists or actors. Photographs allow people to make stereotypical judgements about you, and add little or nothing to your application.
- Do not include any sort of failure, be it your marriage, business, or being asked to leave a job.
- Try to keep your CV to two pages of A4 if possible; this will help you select only relevant entries.
- Ensure there is plenty of 'white space' around your CV so it does not look cramped.
- Use a clean modern font style such as Arial or Verdana, and choose a point size which is easy to read, minimum 11 point. Avoid fancy patterns and borders.
- Check your draft thoroughly for spelling and grammatical errors. When you are happy give it to someone else to check over and provide you with feedback. Remember, you will be amending your CV to meet the requirements of each particular job vacancy.
- Print out your CVs on a high-quality laser printer using good white, not coloured, paper. Do all your hard work justice. Do not be tempted to send out poor quality photocopies, stuffed into an envelope that is too small.
- Make sure you update your generic CV at least twice a year.

Completing your application

Application forms

Many organisations, of course, prefer to issue a standard application form to help them make an initial selection. This is often the first point of contact between the applicant and the prospective employer or university, so it is important that it is well presented and creates a favourable impression. The principles for marketing yourself in CVs also apply to application forms and covering letters. However, application forms provide a further challenge in that you have to fit the breadth of your experience into a set template.

Some forms also have a daunting open page for you to complete, in which you should write a supporting statement. This is your chance to promote yourself to the organisations. So think about why you are making the application and what you can offer in terms of skills or personal qualities that will support it. If no guidance is given, this section could include evidence of relevant skills and qualities, specific achievements and information about your career motivation. This will depend on the job specification. You will find some more ideas in the section following on writing a letter of application.

Here are some helpful points to remember:

- Read the whole application form carefully before you start to complete it. Make sure you understand fully what each question is looking for, how to provide a spread of evidence from across your work, life and study in your answers, and note all the word restrictions and instructions.
- Use a separate sheet of paper or, if possible, a photocopy of the form to plan your answers in full. Complete a draft of all the answers first.
- Often the form will request that you use a black pen, as this aids photocopying for short listing and interview panels. Never change the colour of ink you are using half-way through.
- If you are typing the form, always use a standard font such as Verdana or Arial, and do not set the size less than 11 points. Check it is acceptable to type on the form, and you are not required to complete it by hand.
- If you are handwriting your application form, use a legible, clear style and always make sure it has no spelling or grammatical errors.
- If you are applying directly online on employers' websites, do not alter the size or format of the employer's form unless you are clearly given that option.
- Answer all the questions fully. If you find that there is insufficient room to give a full answer it may be acceptable to continue on a blank sheet of paper that can be attached to the application form.
- Do not be tempted to cut corners and send a CV as a substitute for some questions, unless the form explicitly states this as an option. You are being asked to interpret your experiences to meet the needs of the question.
- Similarly, the temptation to cut and paste answers from previous forms can sometimes backfire on you if, for example, the question is slightly different. Employers may notice and are rarely impressed.
- Never leave questions unanswered, if they are not relevant put 'N/A' (not applicable) to show that they have not been missed.

- Always make sure to complete any enclosed documents such as equal opportunities monitoring or health history forms, if the employer has requested them. Failure to do so might eliminate your application.
- Finally, always retain a photocopy of your application form for yourself after you submit it to the employer. You should bring this with you to the interview.

Writing a letter of application

The main aim of this book is to focus on the study skills you need as a successful degree student. This last chapter has spent time thinking about your future, and in particular has concentrated on producing an excellent application form and CV. This section will consider what you should include in a covering letter. It is outside the remit of this text to coach you for an interview, whether it is for an HE place or a new job, but there are useful sources of information at the end of the chapter.

The purpose of your letter of application is to get the recipient to read not only your CV, but to see you as a potential candidate for the post or the course. There are several key points you should consider:

- Make sure you address your recipient correctly. A personal approach is always preferable, use their correct title and their last name. Do not forget to use 'Yours sincerely' at the end.
- In your first paragraph you should state why you are writing to them. If the position was advertised, state where you saw the advertisement, mention the position title and say you are including your CV. For a speculative letter state the kind of work you are seeking.
- In the main body of the letter tell the recipient something about your career to date, which will get their interest and build on the information in your CV. It might be an area you specialise in, or a particular relevant interest you have developed while studying for your degree. Explain why you are interested in this type of work or area of study, so you can demonstrate an understanding of what it is likely to involve.
- Next concentrate on the skills you have developed, from working and from your experience as a student. If you are applying for a job make sure you cover all the skills mentioned in the advertisement and use positive adjectives like 'well developed', and 'strong', to quantify your statements where possible. You need to make it easy for the recruiter to match you against any person specification they may have.
- The final paragraph should ask for the opportunity of a meeting to further the application and indicate your availability to attend an interview.
- Check the letter for spelling and grammatical errors, and that it expresses your enthusiasm and evidence of research into the position and organisation.
- Generally the letter should be typed in the same font as your CV with an original signature. Occasionally you may be asked to write a covering letter by hand; if so you should comply with this request.

Your next steps on the road of lifelong learning . . .

We are, of course, aware that for many people their working or personal lives do not progress along continuous, upward paths. For some a career has breaks and subsequent returns to paid employment; sideways moves both within and outside organisations; or switches from employment to self-employment and retraining for different careers. Therefore personal planning is not something you do once and then forget. Rather, it is an attitude towards your future. We hope this book has instilled the importance of this attitude. We both hope this book has given you the knowledge, skills and confidence to achieve your personal and career development goals and that the information continues to be of use to you throughout your life.

All the best for your future success.

References and further reading

www.connexions-direct.com – this site is aimed at young people aged 13 to 19 but includes a useful jobs4u careers database.

www.learndirect-advice.co.uk – provides career assessments that generate job suggestions and a great deal of useful job-hunting information. This is a free service but you need to register to use it.

www.niace.org.uk – the website of the National Institute of Adult Continuing Education that advances the interests of adult learners.

www.prospects.ac.uk – an excellent and comprehensive site for HE students. This should be your first port of call. To get the maximum value you need to register to use the full range of services.

www.windmillsprogramme.com – offers a comprehensive range of exercises and activities based on seven tactics for success developed by the University of Liverpool's Graduate Into Employment Unit.

Bibliography

Baume, D. (2003) *Supporting Portfolio Development*, York: Learning and Teaching Support Network Generic Centre.

Bell, J. (2005) *Doing Your Research Project: A Guide for First-Time Researchers in Education and Social Science* (4th Edition), Buckingham: Oxford University Press.

Birley, G. and Moreland, N. (1998) *A Practical Guide to Academic Research*, London: Kogan Page.

Burchfield, H.W. (2004) *The New Fowler's Modern English Usage*, Oxford: Oxford University Press.

Buzan, T. (2006) *Brilliant Memory: unlock the power of your mind*, Harlow: BBC Active.

Clarke, K. (2007) *ILE Learning and Teaching Projects 2006–2007*, Wolverhampton: Wolverhampton University.

Cohen, L., Manion, L. and Morrison, K. (2000) *Research Methods in Education* (5th Edition), London: Routledge & Falmer.

Cottrell, S. (2003) *Skills for Success: The Personal Development Planning Handbook*, Basingstoke: Palgrave Macmillan.

Covey, S., Merrill, A.R. and Merrill, R.A. (1994) *First Things First*, London: Simon and Schuster.

Cowan, J. (1998) *On Becoming An Innovative University Teacher: reflection in action*, Buckingham: Society for Research into Higher Education and Open University Press.

Denzin, N. and Lincoln, Y. (eds) (2000) *Handbook of Qualitative Research* (2nd Edition), London: Sage.

Elliott, J. (2002) 'What is applied research in education?' in *Building Research Capacity*, Issue 3.

Eysenbach, G. and Till, J.E. (2001) 'Ethical issues in qualitative research on internet communities', *British Medical Journal* 323 (7321), 1103–5.

Foddy, W. (1995) *Constructing Questions for Interviews and Questionnaires*, Cambridge: Cambridge University Press.

Gardner, H. (1983) *Frames of Mind*, New York: Harper Collins.

Glaser, B. and Strauss, A. (1967) *The Discovery of Grounded Theory*, Chicago: Aldine.

Goby, V. P. and Lewis, J. H. (2000) 'The Key Role of Listening in Business: a study of the Singapore insurance industry', *Business Communication Quarterly*, 63 (2) 41–51.

Gray, D., Cundell, S., Hay, D. and O'Neill, J. (2004) *Learning through the Workplace: a guide to work-based learning*, Cheltenham: Nelson Thornes.

Greenhill, A. and Fletcher, G. (eds) (2003) *Electronic references and scholarly citations of internet sources* [online] available from: www.spaceless.com/WWWVL/ [accessed 14/08/08].

Bibliography

Jarvis, P. (1992) *The Paradoxes of Learning*, San Francisco, CA: Jossey-Bass.

King, G. (2004) *Collins Good Punctuation Guide,* Glasgow: HarperCollins.

Kolb, D.A. (1984) *Experiential Learning: experience as a source of learning and development,* Englewood Cliffs, New Jersey: Prentice Hall.

Lashley, C. and Best, W. (2001) *12 Steps to Study Success*, London and New York: Continuum.

Long, M., Ferrier, F. and Heagney, M. (2006) *Stay, Play or Give it Away? Students changing or leaving university study in the first year*, Melbourne: Centre for the Economics of Training, Monash University.

MacRae, C. (2007) 'Using sense to make sense of art: young children in art galleries', *Early Years*, Vol. 27.2, 159–170.

McMillan, J. (2005) *Course Change and Attrition from Higher Education (Longitudinal Surveys of Australian Youth, Research Report 39)*, Melbourne: Australian Council for Educational Research.

Megginson, D. and Whitaker, V. (2003) *Continuing Professional Development*, London: Chartered Institute of Personnel and Development.

Moon, J.A. (1999) *Reflection in Learning and Professional Development*, London: Routledge Falmer.

Moon, J.A. (2004) *A Handbook of Reflective and Experiential Learning,* London: Routledge & Falmer.

Moon, J. A. (2006) *Learning Journals: a handbook for academics, students and professional development,* London: Kogan Page.

Nixon, N., Smith, K., Stafford, S. and Camm, S. (2006) *Work-based Learning: illuminating the higher education landscape*, Report by KSA Partnership for The Higher Education Academy, York: Higher Education Academy.

Patton, M. (1990) *Qualitative Evaluation and Research Methods* (2nd Edition), London: Sage.

Petrass, M. (1999) *Effective Listening Skills: an examination of what skills make for a good listener*, London: Museums and Libraries and Archives Council.

QAA (2001) *The Framework for Higher Education Qualifications,* Gloucester: Quality Assurance Agency.

Robson, C. (2002) *Real World Research* (2nd Edition), Oxford, UK: Blackwell Publishing.

Rowntree, D. (1976) *Learn to Study* (2nd Edition), London: Macdonald and Co.

Rudd, D. (2004) *Giving a presentation*, available from http://data.bolton.ac.uk/learning/helpguides/studyskills/present.pdf.

Stephen, M. (2006) *Teach Yourself Basic Computer Skills*, London: McGraw-Hill.

Trask, R.L. (1997) *The Penguin Guide to Punctuation,* London: Penguin.

Trask, R.L. (2000) *The Penguin Dictionary of English Grammar,* London: Penguin.

Trochim, W. (2005) *Ethics in Research*, London: Sage.

Truss, L. (2003) *Eats, Shoots & Leaves: the zero tolerance approach to punctuation,* London: Profile Books.

White, B. (2003) *Dissertation Skills for Business and Management Students,* London: Thomson Learning.

Wilson, E. and Bedford, D. (2008) '"New Partnerships for Learning": teachers and teaching assistants working together in schools – the way forward', *Journal of Education for Teaching*, 34:2, 137–150.

Woodley, A. (2004) *Earning, Learning and Paying: the results from a national survey of the costs of financing of part-time students in higher education*, Research Report 600 for the Department for Education and Skills, London: Open University.

Wyse, D. (2006) *The Good Writing Guide for Education Students*. London: Sage Publishing.

Yorke, M. and Longden, B. (2008) *The First Year Experience of Higher Education in the UK: final report*, York: The Higher Education Academy.

Websites

www.ase-solutions.co.uk – the website of Assessment for Selection and Employment

www.ask.com – a major search engine

www.bbc.co.uk/learning/basic_skills.shtml – an excellent BBC site, offers online learning addressing a range of skills at different levels

www.bbc.co.uk/radio/podcasts/directory/

www.bbc.co.uk/skillswise – BBC site which aims to enable adults to improve their basic reading, writing and number skills

www.bbc.co.uk/webwise – for free online learning course

www.blogger.com – a hosted blogging platform

www.bloglines.com – Bloglines, a search engine

www.blogscope.net – BlogScope, another search engine

www.bl.uk – The British Library

www.britsoc.co.uk/equality – British Sociological Association's guidelines on non-discriminatory language

www.brunel.ac.uk/learnhigher/participating-in-seminars

http://bubl.ac.uk – Bulletin Board for Libraries – (BUBL) a multi-subject gateway

www.cemp.ac.uk/research/reflectivelearning – Centre for Excellence in Media Practice

http://clusty.com – meta-search engine

www.connexions-direct.com – this site is aimed at young people aged 13 to 19 but includes a useful jobs4u careers database

http://danwilton.com/eportfolios – an e-portfolios portal

http://del.icio.us – a social bookmarking site

www.dogpile.com – a meta-search engine

www.education.ex.ac.uk/dll/studyskills/note_taking_skills.htm – hints for taking notes from lectures

http://elgg.net – provides e-learning portfolio software

www.eportfolios.ac.uk – provides advice on developing e-portfolios

www.flickr.com – a social networking site for presenting e-portfolios visually

www.glos.ac.uk/departments/lis/referencing/footnotes/

www.google.com – probably the largest search engine

hsc.uwe.ac.uk/dataanalysis/quantWhat.asp

www.inspiringlearningforall.gov.uk/measuring_learning/steps_in_the_process/analyse_data/

www.intute.ac.uk – a multi-subject gateway

www.intute.ac.uk/socialsciences – useful papers on qualitative analysis

www.jisclegal.ac.uk – for a full explanation of intellectual property rights

www.jiscmail.ac.uk – Joint Information Systems Committee

www.kartoo.com – meta-search engine

www.keyskillssupport.net

www.learndirect-advice.co

www.learning-styles-online.com – provides an analysis of learning styles

www.leeds.ac.uk/library/training/referencing

www.movabletype.org – Movable Type, a blogging platform

www.niace.org.uk – the website of the National Institute of Adult Continuing Education

http://news.bbc.co.uk, BBC News

www.open.ac.uk/inclusiveteaching/pages/inclusive-teaching/discussions-groupwork-and-presentations.php

www.open.ac.uk/safari/

www.open.gov.uk – UK government reports

http://openlearn.open.ac.uk/studyskills

www.prospects.ac.uk

www.qaa.ac.uk/academicinfrastructure/benchmark

www.qaa.ac.uk/academicinfrastructure/FHEQ

www.rdg.ac.uk/studyskills

www.recordingachievement.org – Centre for Recording Achievement

http://scholar.google.co.uk/ – Google Scholar, a multi-subject gateway

www.search.yahoo.com

http://spaces.live.com – MSN Spaces, a hosted blogging platform

www.statistics.gov.uk – National Statistics Online

www.support4learning.org.uk

www.technorati.com

www.windmillsprogramme.com

www.worcester.ac.uk/studyskills

http://wordpress.org – WordPress, a blogging platform

Glossary

Abstract	A piece of writing at the start of a document which summarises for the reader what the work contains.
Acronym	The practice of using either the initials or word formed from the initials in place of a full title. For example, APEL stands for Accreditation of Prior Experiential Learning.
Action research	A form of research method which takes place within a practitioner's working practice. It is cyclical and the findings of the first stage are incorporated into the next stage and reflected upon.
Analyse	To examine data or text to reduce it to its basic elements.
Anonymity	In research this means it is not possible to identify person(s) and/or place(s) from the data.
Appendix	Additional supporting material included at the end of an extended piece of writing.
Assessment criteria	Descriptors of the skills, knowledge and understanding which must be attained and demonstrated to achieve a level or grade.
Bibliography	A list in alphabetical order of all texts, journals, web and online material consulted to prepare a book, paper, presentation and so on.
Blog	A contraction of the word 'weblog', a website usually maintained by an individual, with regular entries of commentary and other materials such as pictures and video.
Citation	An academic convention where one acknowledges a quotation, reference to or use of another person's work in their own.
Cognition	Knowing and understanding.
Colloquialism	A word, phrase or expression characteristic of ordinary or familiar conversation rather than formal speech or writing.
Competencies	The description of behaviours, knowledge or actions needed to perform a role.
Conception	Or concept formation, deep understanding which can be recalled when needed.

Curriculum Vitae	A statement of your qualifications, employment and training experience together with other data relevant to application for a position or further training.
Data	A collection of information based on experience, observation, experiment and so on from which conclusions might be drawn.
DDC	Dewey Decimal Classification, a decimal classification system commonly used in libraries.
Deductive research	Where the research attempts to provide a proposed answer to a question.
Discriminatory	To unfavourably distinguish a difference.
ECDL	European Computer Driving Licence, IT skills qualification at level 2.
Ellipsis	Three dots in a quotation signifying that words in the original have been omitted.
EndNote	An electronic bibliographic management system.
Endnotes	Notes placed at the end of a chapter to amplify or reference points identified in the text.
Ethics	Guiding principles about appropriate behaviour in dealing with others.
Ethnographic	A social science research method which relies on the researcher becoming very close to the subject they are studying.
Explicit knowledge	Knowledge which has been articulated or codified, such as through a lecture or a textbook.
Footnotes	Notes at the bottom of a page to amplify or reference an identified point in the text.
Generic	Characteristic of large group, class and so on.
Hawthorne effect	Where the behaviour of subjects investigated for research changes as a result of being observed without there being any intervention.
Hermeneutics	Interpreting and studying linguistic and non-linguistic expressions.
Homophones	Words which have the same sound as another. For example, bear/bare.
Hypothesis	An answer to a problem is proposed.
ICT	Information and Communications Technology.
Inductive research	Where the researcher formulates questions to find answers to a problem.

Intellectual property rights	The creator of written work, a painting, a poem and so on has the right to control how the work is used.
Interquartile range	Where the first and last quarters of a data set are ignored.
JISC	The Joint Information Systems Committee, an independent advisory body on the use of ICT in education.
Literature review	Critical analysis of published knowledge about a topic. It is summarised and compared with other research studies, theoretical papers and so on.
Mean	Or average, where the data is added together and divided by the number of entries.
Median	The mid-way value when a data set is ordered.
Methodology	The rationale and assumptions made in the selection of appropriate research methods.
Mode	The value(s) which occur most frequently in a data set.
Moodle	An open-source Virtual Learning Environment (VLE).
OPAC	Online Public Access Catalogue, an online catalogue of materials held in a library.
Parameter	Boundary which is constant for the particular case.
Parentheses	Round brackets.
Personal attributes	Qualities specific to a person. Used in business to identify suitability for a position.
Phenomenological	Research which emphasises the importance of how people feel and experience things.
Plagiarism	The intentional or unintentional use of another person's work as if it were your own.
Podcast	Digital audio files which can be downloaded from the internet and listened to via a mobile device.
Portfolio	Structured collection comprising labelled evidence of your learning and critical reflection on it. Note there are slight variations in the way this term is used.
Practitioner research	Research carried out in a place of employment by someone who works there with a view to understanding and improving practice. Sometimes linked to action research.

Procedural knowledge	Knowledge gained by doing something repeatedly.
Professional association	Organisation which furthers the interests of particular professions; includes trades unions.
Provenance	The place of origin, authenticity and authorship of something.
QAA	Quality Assurance Agency, a government agency that reviews the standards and quality of higher education in the UK.
QCA	Quality and Curriculum Authority, a regulatory body which maintains and develops the national curriculum and associated assessments, tests and examinations.
Qualitative research	A research method, mostly using words, to present conclusions which aims to find out what people say, think and do.
Quantitative research	A research method where data is presented numerically.
Quotation	The use of another person's words in your text.
Rapporteur	Person(s) appointed to report back at the end of a seminar, lecture, meeting or similar.
Reference Manager	An electronic bibliographic management system.
References	All books, journals, web and online material you have referred to in your work. Usually listed in alphabetical order at the end.
Reflective learning	Reflecting objectively on learning experience with a view to understanding and making changes.
Reliability	The extent to which a method used to obtain results would produce the same results under identical conditions.
Research	The process of gathering, analysing and drawing conclusions from data.
Respondent	Someone who takes part in research.
Sampling	The selection of people, places or things to investigate for research. There are many ways in which a sample can be chosen.
Scanning	Reading very quickly to get an overview before reading in depth.
SCONUL	Society of College, National and University Libraries, maintains a reciprocal access scheme granting borrowing rights to other libraries.

Seminar	Scheduled discussion group accompanying a lecture series. Intended to consolidate learning. Students may present prepared tasks.
Skills	Learned capacity or talent to carry out predetermined tasks, often with the minimum outlay of time and energy.
Skimming	Letting your eyes move quickly over a text to pick out key words or phrases.
SPSS	A statistical software package to analyse large sets of data (originally Statistical Package for Social Sciences).
Suffix	An addition of syllables at the end of a word which add to or changes its meaning. For example, mean/meaningful.
Superscript	Text or numbers usually in smaller script above the level of the main text to identify that there is a matching note or reference, either as a footnote or endnote.
Tacit knowledge	Unconscious or intuitive learning.
Theoretical framework	Interrelated ideas and concepts about a topic which underpin the new research.
Theoretical knowledge	That which is gained from academic study.
Triangulation	The practice of using more than one data collection method or researcher to cross-check findings and increase validity.
URL	Uniform Resource Locator, a website's unique address on the internet.
Validity	Whether the data obtained measures what it is supposed to be measuring.
VARK	An acronym for identifying preferred learning styles, standing for Visual, Auditory, Reading/Writing and Kinaesthetic.
Visual stimuli	That which attracts the eye.
VLE	Virtual Learning Environment. This is an integrated environment of all the online tools you will need for studying and may include course information, online resources, email and discussion boards, blogs, wikis, podcasts, instant messaging and video-conferencing.
Wiki	A website that can be built collaboratively by a group. Wikipedia is probably the best-known example.

Index

abbreviations 132
absorb 161
analysing qualitative data 81, 93–5
  content analysis 96–7
  discourse analysis 97–8
  using computer software for analysis
    95–6
analysing quantitative data 81, 98–100
anthropologists, ethnographic research 86
application, learning and 7
aptitude tests 23
Ask.com (www.ask.com) 55
Assessment for Selection and
    Employment (ASE)
    (www.ase-solutions.co.uk) 24
Athens account 60, 115
Athens password 77
Atlas-ti, software for visual qualitative
    analysis 96
auditing your experiences 169, 170
  which personal details should you
      include? 170–1
    gathering information on education,
      training and other interests 171–3
    thinking about your work experience
      173–4
auditing your support network 1, 5–6
auditory, learning through listening 8

barriers to learning 1, 14
Baume, D. 26–7
BBC News (http://news.bbc.co.uk) 58
Bedford D. 102–3, 107, 109–10
Belbin, Meredith, looks at team roles 24
Bell, J. 68
BIDS online bibliographic data-base 115
Blackboard or WebCT 30, 61
'blog', contraction of word 'weblog' 62
blogging platform, specialist software 63
Boolean operators 56
British Library (www.bl.uk) 58

British Psychological Society, tests
    and 23
British Sociological Association,
    guidelines on language 136
Bulletin Board for Libraries
    (http://bulb.ac.uk) 56
Buzan, Tony, *Brilliant Memory: unlock the
    power of your mind* 163

careers advisory service (CAS) 170
CD-R and CD-RW disks, difference
    between 61
checklist of things to take to examination
    room 165
Chicago referencing method 112
choosing an appropriate methodology 81
choosing your research sample 68,
    79–80
Clarke, K. 42
Clusty (http://clusty.com) 55
cognition, level of learning and 7
commonly misspelled words 136
compiling a bibliography 105, 112
  different systems for referencing
      bibliographies 112
    Harvard system 112–14
  referencing electronic sources 114–15
completing your application 169, 178
  application forms 178–9
  next steps on the road to lifelong
      learning 180
  writing a letter of application 179
Computer-Assisted Qualitative Data
    Analysis (CAQDAS) 95
conception, learning and 7
contractions 132
Covey, S., four quadrants of time 11–13
Cowan, J., 'reflection for action' 19
curriculum vitae,
  layout of a chronological CV 175
  layout of a skills based CV 176

data overload 93
databases,
  searchable collections of reference 59
  useful to investigate research 77
descriptive research 79
determining what to research 68, 71–2
  checking if you can manage the
     research 72–3
    are you interested in the topic? 73
    are you ready for change? 73–4
    does the topic fit within the
      expectations of the subject you are
      studying? 73
    is your proposal realistic and
      achievable? 72–3
  formulating and clarifying the research
    74–5
developing your information technology
    skills 54, 65–6
Dewey Decimal Classification system
    (DDC) 37
dictionaries 39
different patterns of work and study 1,
    2–5
Dogpile (www.dogpile.com) 55
drawing conclusions from the data 81,
    102–3
drawing up your revision timetable 160,
    161–4

EBSCO, bibliographic data–base 115
electronic bibliography 105
  management 105, 115
Elliott, J. 98
encyclopaedias 39
Endnote (www.endnote.com) 115
ensuring validity and reliability 68
ethical considerations 68, 75
  some guiding principles 76
expectations of undergraduate level
    writing 120, 121–2
explanatory research 79
exploratory research 79
Eysenbach, G. 91

finding a place and time to study 1, 10
first impressions 93
Flickr(www.flickr.com) 30
footnotes and endnotes 105, 111

Framework for Higher Education
    Qualifications (FHEQ) 122–3
  gaining access to workplace data 68,
    70
  tips to help you gain access 70–1

Gardner, Howard, multiple intelligences 8
generic curriculum vitae (CV) 169
glossary 42, 185–9
Gloucester University website, notes
    about footnotes and endnotes 111
Goby, V.P. 47
Google Scholar
    (http://scholar.google.co.uk/) 56
Google (www.google.com) 55
group presentations 143, 158–9
guide to academic qualifications 121–2

Harvard system of referencing for
    bibliography 112–14
hosted blogging platform, Blogger
    (www.blogger.com) 63
how to avoid plagiarism 105, 116–19
how to cite work in the text 105, 109–110
how to plan an effective presentation
    143, 145
  construction – writing and organising
    the presentation 148–9
  content – researching the topic 148
  context – understanding the parameters
    how long? 147
    what? 147
    when? 147
    where? 147
  context – who is listening and what do
    they want to know? 145–6
  cross-checking 149

'ibid'(short for, ibidem Latin for 'in the
    same place') 110
identifying key points from lectures 34,
    47–8
  making notes 48–9
  recording the lecture as an alternative
    49
  storing your notes 49–50
importance of anti-virus software and
    backups 54, 60
  backing up your pc 60–61

tips to safeguard computer against malware 60
important preparation before the exam 160, 164
  planning an examination strategy 164–5
index, look up key words in 40
index cards 163
index for portfolio 26, 29
information and communications technology (ICT) 54
internal consistency 93
interval scales questionnaires 88
Intute (www.intute.ac.uk) 56, 59
iTunes (www.apple.com/iTunes) 62

Jarvis, P., three states of learning 8–9
Joint Information Systems Committee see JISC
Journal of Education for Teaching 102–3
Juice Receiver (www.juicereceiver.com) 62

KartOO (www.kartoo.com) 55
key instruction words 127–9
keyword tags 59
kinaesthetic, learning through activity 8
Kolb, David, four phases of a 'learning cycle 9

learndirect (www.learndirect-advice, co.uk) 176
learning online in the virtual classroom 54, 61
  blogs 62–3
  discussion boards 64
  netiquette – a guide to good communications using technology 64–5
  podcasting 62
  what is a virtual learning environment(VLE)? 61
  wikis 64
Learning Resources Centre (LRC), e-Book collections, 'invisible web' 59
learning in tutorials, groups and seminars 34, 50
  group work 52
  seminars 51

tutorials 51
Lewis, J.H. 47
log on to http://del.icio.us to set up an account 59
Long, M. 4
Longden, B. 5
looking at available support for improving basic skills 34, 52–3

McMillan, J. 5
MacRea, C. 117
making notes and effective summaries of texts 34, 43–4
  coping with unfamiliar words and complex sentences 47
  reasons for making notes 45
  techniques for note–making
    concept maps or 'sprays' 46
    double notes 45
    grids, tables, flowcharts and timelines 46
    headings and bullet points 45
    linear notes 46
    notes on handouts or texts 45
making your presentation 143, 156
  final checks 156–7
  the presentation 157–8
managing morale and motivation 1, 14–16
managing the writing process for producing assignments 120, 124–6
memory stick 12
mentor, ideal is usually a more experienced colleague 9
Microsoft office, look at templates and CV wizard 177
Microsoft Outlook 18
Modern Languages Association (MLA) 112
Morrisby organization (www.morrisby.co.uk) 24
Movable Type (www.movabletype.org) 63
Myers-Briggs Type Indicator (MBTI) 24

National Statistics Online (www.statistics.gov.uk) 59
National Vocational Qualification 26, 59
'New partnerships for learning' 102
nominal questionnaires 88

Index

Non-Numerical Unstructured Data:
Indexing (Microsoft NUD*IST 95
NVivo and N4 for Mac, qualitative data
analysis and 95

Online Public Access Catalogue (OPAC)
38
'op.cit.' (short for *opus citatum* 'The work
quoted') 110
Open University's OpenLearn
(http://openlearn.open.ac.uk) 66
ordinal or likert questionnaires 88
over-confidence 93

Patton, M. 92
participating in seminars and tutorials
143, 144–5
PDA (Personal Digital Assistant) 18
PDFs, Word or Excel documents 55
PebblePad (www.pebblelearning) 30–31
personal development planning (PDP) 17,
22
analyse your job description and person
specification 24
analyse your transferable skills 24–5
define yourself through psychometric
testing 23–4
drawing up your own personal
development plan 25–6
some ideas for developing your own
PDP 22–3
personality tests 24
Petrass, M. 47
plagiarism, failure to acknowledge
sources 105
Post-it flag 41
PowerPoint presentations 155
preliminary issues 68, 69
preparing for your first essay 120, 126
analyse the question 126–9
producing an essay plan 130–1
presentation, pointers for success 157–8
presenting the findings 81, 100–102
primary data 92
process of writing your essay 120, 136
coping with writer's block 139
essential checklist before submission of
any written work 140

learning from feedback 140
writing a concluding paragraph 138
writing the main body of your essay
137–8
writing your opening paragraph 136–7
writing your second draft 139
producing a Professional Development
Portfolio 17
an APEL portfolio 32
checklist for submission of portfolio 31
collecting the evidence 28–9
continuing professional development
portfolio 32
creating an e-portfolio 30–31
different types of portfolio 26
portfolio for assessment 27
portfolio for development 26–7
portfolio as repository 26
think about structure 29–30
using your portfolio after you have
finished your degree, portfolios
to support
presentations for interviews 31–2
what to include 27–8
writing a critical commentary 30
Prospects website (www.prospects.ac.uk)
24

QAA webside (www.qaa.ac.uk/
academicinfrastructure/benchmark)
25
QAA website (www.qaa.ac.uk/
academicinfrastructure/FHEQ) 121
'Quadrant of Deception', here we are
meeting other people's priorities 12
'Quadrant of Necessity', time on urgent
important tasks 12
'Quadrant of Quality', we should spend
most time in this quadrant 11
'Quadrant of Waste', activities here are
neither urgent nor important 12
Qualifications and Curriculum Authority
(QCA) (www.qca.org.uk) 25
qualitative data collection methods 81,
83
case study 83
ethnographic study 86–7
grounded theory 86

group interviews 85
hermeneutics 87
interviews 83–4
observation 85–6
phenomenological research 87
single person interviews 84–5
telephone interviews 85
qualitative and quantitative data
    collection, differences between 82
Quality Assurance Agency (QAA),
    Guidelines for HE Progress Files 17, 66
    two frameworks for HE qualifications
        121
quantitative data collection methods 81,
    87–9
    action research 91
    diaries 92
    experiments 90
    online research 90–1
    other less usual methods, documentary
        or content analysis 91–2
    questionnaires 88
    surveys 87–8
quotation in the text 105, 106–7
    including visual material 108–9
    incorporating quotations into your
        writing 107
    quoting numerical data 108

ranked responses in questionnaires 89
raw data 108
read/write, learning through the written
        word 8
reading effectively 34
    reading for information 41–2
    skimming and scanning 40–1
    what kind of reader are you? 43
ready-made asynchronous groups,
        hosted by JISC 64
Record of Achievement (RoA) 26
Reference Manager (www.refman.com)
        115
reflective writing 17, 18
    reflection on your own personal
        development 21–2
    setting the parameters 18–19
    shaping the journal to suit you –
        possible ideas for structure

in form of a diary 20
    in terms of issues and themes 20–21
    what could your reflective writing
        include? 19–20
relax 161
remember 161
replenish 161
reviewing the literature 68, 76–8
    ensuring validity and reliability 78–9
Robson, C. 69, 76–9, 87, 90, 93, 113
Rudd, D. 157

sample marking scheme 124–5
Saville and Holdsworth
        (www/shlgroup.com) 24
Schön, Donald, on reflection 18
SCONUL agreement
        www/access.sconul.ac.uk/members
        38
secondary data 92
semantic differential in questionnaires 89
semi-structured interviews 83
Skills4Study, PDP resources for students
        22
slang words 132
SMART goals 25
sources which should be acknowledged
        118
speed reading exercise
        (www.bbc.co.uk/skillswise) 41
split infinitives 133
statistics as data 108
stress management 160–1
structured interviews 83
'study buddy' 163
SWOT analysis 22–3
Synchronous and asynchronous
        discussions 64

techniques for exam success 160, 166
    dealing with exam anxiety 167
    presentation of your answers 167
    review all your answers to maximise
        marks 167–8
    select the best questions for you 166
    time management for examinations
        166–7
technorati.com 63

telephone surveys 88
the research process 68, 71
think laterally 77–8
Till, J.E. 91
time management 1, 11–14
timetable, mapping out your week a day
    at a time 11
Truss, Lynne, *Eats, Shoots & Leaves* 133
Turnitin, anti-plagiatism software 111

UK government reports
    (www.open.gov.uk) 59
understanding your learning style 1, 7–9
understanding generic assessment
    criteria and marking schemes 120,
    122–4
uneven reliability 93
Uniform Resource Locator (URL) 57
University of Wolverhampton 42
unstructured interviews 84
USB flash drive 61
using audio visual aids 143, 150
  artefacts 154
  computer simulations and online
      presentations 152–3
  flip charts and whiteboards 152
  handouts 155
  interactive whiteboards 153
  overhead transparencies (OHTs) 151–2
  radio and television (including CDs,
      DVDs and video) 150–51
  slide projector transparencies 154
using and citing electronic material 105,
    110–111
using the internet and electronic
    resources 54, 55
  downloadable articles and books
      59–60
  finding the right search tool 55
  judging the quality of the information
      58
  organising information using social
      bookmarks 59
  planning your search strategy 56–7
  provenance – who is providing the
      information and how reliable are
      they? 57–8
  subject gateways 56

timeliness – when was the information
    written? 58–9
using the Learning Resources Centre 34,
    35
  finding a book 37–8
  using the internet and electronic
      sources 39–40
  using journals and newspapers 39
  what can you usually expect to find?
      35–7
using PowerPoint and other technology
    143, 155–6
using your careers service 169–70
using your workplace as a source of
    learning 9–10

Vancouver referencing system for
    bibliographies 112
VARK acronym, way we process
    information 7–8
Virtual Learning Environment (VLE)
    facilities 54, 61
  Blackboad or WebCT 30
visual, way of learning 8

web-based feed reader, My Yahoo or
    Google Reader 62
why develop presentation skills? 143–4
why you need to cite your sources 105,
    106
Wikipedia (www.wikipedia.org) 58, 62
Wilson, E. 102–3, 107, 109
Woodley, A. 1, 14
WordPress (http://wordpress.org) 30, 63
World Wide Web (www) 55
writing for academic purposes – some
    practical guidance 120, 131
  always write in complete sentences
      133
  avoid colloquialisms and slang 132–3
  avoid discriminatory language 136
  capital letters 133
  other punctuations marks 134–5
  spelling 135–6
  take care with emphasis 132
  understand how to punctuate 133
  use of personal pronouns 131–2
writing a professional CV 169, 174

chronological or skills-based CV 174–5
the optional personal profile summary
    175–7
some final words of advice 177
writing reports and dissertations 120,
    140–1
    writing a dissertation or research report
    141
        after the findings you could add 142
        after the introduction you could add
        141
        after recommendations 142
www.bbc.co.uk/webwise/learn, free basic
    guide to using the internet 65

www.learning-styles-online.com,
    questionnaire on 22
www.open.ac.uk/safari/, free from Open
    University 66
www.prospects.ac.uk, UK's official
    graduate careers website 176
www.teamtechnology.co.uk 24
Wyse, D. 42

Yahoo! Search (search.yahoo.com) 55
Yorke, M. 5
YouTube (http://uk.youtube.com) 30